The Talking Cure

The Talking Cure

The Science
Behind Psychotherapy

Susan C. Vaughan, M.D.

A Grosset/Putnam Book
Published by G. P. Putnam's Sons
New York

All the patients that appear in this book are composites drawn from my clinical
work. Names and details have been changed to protect confidentiality.

A Grosset/Putnam Book
Published by G. P. Putnam's Sons
Publishers Since 1838
200 Madison Avenue
New York, NY 10016

Library of Congress Cataloging-in-Publication Data

Vaughan, Susan C.
The talking cure : the science behind psychotherapy /
by Susan C. Vaughan.
p.   cm.
Includes bibliographical references and index.
ISBN 0-399-14229-0
1. Psychodynamic psychotherapy—Physiological aspects.
2. Neural circuitry—Adaptation. 3. Mind and body. I. Title.
RC489.P72V38   1997
616.89'14—dc21   96-45237 CIP

This book is printed on acid-free paper. ∞

Printed in the United States of America

1   3   5   7   9   10   8   6   4   2

Book design by Iris Weinstein

Acknowledgments

In the preparation of this manuscript, I was fortunate to have the advice of several colleagues who read the material and offered invaluable suggestions. They were Steven Roose, Stanley Bone, Elizabeth Auchincloss, Myron Hofer, David Olds, and Roger MacKinnon. In addition, I would like to thank my many teachers at Harvard College, Columbia College of Physicians and Surgeons, the New York State Psychiatric Institute, and the Columbia Department of Psychiatry. I am most grateful to my supervisors and teachers at the Columbia Center for Psychoanalytic Training and Research, especially Roger MacKinnon and Steven Roose, for teaching me what I know about the mind and for encouraging my research efforts, as well as to Ron Rieder, who helped me find ways to do what I wanted to do after residency. I have spent the past twelve years at Columbia, and it has become

Acknowledgments

my intellectual home, with a wonderful atmosphere that promotes congenial debate and the free exchange of ideas.

The idea for *The Talking Cure* grew out of late-night conversations with Elizabeth Stone, a writer who encouraged me to write about my views of mind and brain in a way that would be comprehensible to nonexperts. In essence, Elizabeth gave me the idea for the book she wanted to read herself, then supported me throughout the process as I went off and wrote it. My agent, Joy Harris, believed in me and the book and didn't stop until she had shepherded me through the proposal process and found the perfect editor for me. That editor, Jane Isay, had the "gleam in her eye" that let her see what the project could become, and she guided my organization and remained attuned with me and my ideas throughout the process of writing and editing. Her assistant, Kate Murphy, made helpful comments on various drafts of the book and conveyed her excitement about the project throughout; her efficiency made the many logistical details manageable. Martha Ramsey's excellent copyediting helped to ensure that the science in the book was as clear as possible.

I would literally not be myself without the loving attention and support of my parents, Chester and Norma Vaughan, and my analytic parents, Robert Glick and Jane Asch. There are not words that adequately express my gratitude.

I am also enormously indebted to my patients, whose minds I have learned about because of their courage in sharing their innermost thoughts and feelings with me. In par-

Acknowledgments

ticular, I want to thank Walter S. Katz, who reminded me of why I became a doctor and who taught me that even when talking is not a cure, it can be a tremendous relief.

Finally, Deb Wasser's love, support, and belief in me over the past eleven years have provided an invaluable base from which creativity and synthesis could take flight.

For Deb

Contents

Preface

When patients ask how psychotherapy is supposed to work and what it is supposed to do for them, too often they get the Wizard-of-Oz routine. Their therapists, ensconced securely behind a velvet curtain of intimidating silence and anonymity, often do not encourage them to pursue their questions further. I wrote this book because I believe that patients deserve to know as much as I do about how psychotherapy works. And we are finally in a position to apply some interesting findings from fields such as artificial intelligence, neurobiology, infant observation, and psychotherapy research that can help us understand the psychotherapeutic process. Perhaps most important, we now know that psychotherapy directly affects the brain. That's right, the brain. If you're tired of "Listening to Prozac," let me tell you about "Talking to Neurons."

Preface

Psychotherapy works because it produces long-lasting changes in the neurons that make up your mind. And that's a message that still is lost to most people pursuing psychotherapy, patients as well as therapists. So if you've got the spirit of inquiry to see how people really change their minds through hard work within the intimate and emotional relationship between patient and therapist, follow me. I promise that the view we now can construct of how psychotherapy changes the brain is more multifaceted and dazzling than a visit to the Land of Oz. And if you thought the talking cure was obsolete, let me pull the curtain on the psychotherapeutic endeavor. When I do, you won't see a cowering little man pretending to be powerful, but—voilà!—the splendid wizardry of mind and brain together in action.

1

Putting the Neuron
Back in Neurosis

I dreamed I was at your office. I was sad that it was the end of our session, the last one before I go away on my trip. As I was leaving, I accidentally jarred a glass table by the door. I saw the sheet of glass fall off the table—in slow motion. I wanted to catch the edge, but I couldn't move. The glass hit the ground and shattered into thousands of shards. I was afraid to look at you. I thought you would be very angry. When I finally looked up I saw that a gash on your right palm was bleeding. I felt scared and sad.

I find myself glancing anxiously at my right palm as Katie tells me her dream, and then I wonder, why right? I feel for a moment like the Freudian analyst in the *New Yorker* cartoon: his patient says, "Good morning," and he thinks, "I wonder what he meant by that?" But as I think about it, I realize that it is my custom, when there is to be a break in treatment, to shake hands with Katie at the end of the session and wish her well. The handshake is a rare moment of physical contact in a treatment that stresses putting thoughts and feelings into words. In a way it seems paradoxical, the formality of the gesture juxtaposed with the intimacy of our relationship. My patients may not know how I take my coffee, but they do know me, or at least what I think of as the essence of me: how I think about life, love, loss, relationships. I wonder if the gash on my palm would somehow prevent me from reaching out to Katie as she left. If the handshake helps to solidify her sense of connectedness to me as we part, would Katie wind up leaving me mad and hurt instead?

These thoughts run through my mind, but I say nothing and wait to hear what Katie will say about the dream images. She notes, breathing a sigh of relief, that I do not actually have a glass table in my office. She speaks of our impending separation, ruminating about whether she will be able to make a successful presentation at an important meeting on her business trip. She jokes that she wishes I were coming with her in her suitcase, saying that she would feel more sure of her abilities if I were with her.

But having expressed this wish to carry me with her, Katie herself begins to realize that her joke has led us right back to a topic we have been focusing on recently, her relationship with her mother in her teenage years. She recalls, more solemnly, that she did in fact hurt her mother as she grew up and became more independent, by literally and figuratively leaving her mother behind. "She needed me to need her," she reiterates, somewhat angrily. "She would get her most depressed, angry, and withdrawn when it came time for me to leave her, like to go to camp or to college. She would always say she didn't want to get in my way, that she wanted to let go of me when the time came, but I think it was hard for her."

"Do you think our impending separation relates somehow to the image of the shattering glass in the dream?" I ask. Katie pauses for a moment, then says, "My mother used to say that I was like a bull in a china shop, barreling around the house. I was too much for her, energetic and lively as a child. I guess that same energy ultimately propelled me away from her, into a career that involved my moving far from home." She looks quizzical for a moment. "Oh, and there's a story I remember that really involved broken glass." Although I am always eager to hear such stories, I find myself momentarily distracted, caught back at the idea of Katie as a bull in a china shop.

I am a microsurgeon of the mind. A physician, psychiatrist, and psychoanalyst by training, I use words and symbols to explore and change the neural landscape of my patients' minds and brains the way a surgeon uses a scalpel to expose and excise problematic structures in the body. You may be wondering why a psychoanalyst should talk like a brain surgeon. After all, psychotherapy is not neurosurgery. Or is it? It's my intention in this book to show how and why intensive, psychoanalytically oriented psychotherapy changes your brain and in so doing alters the makeup of your mind.

Let me say at the outset that in calling psychotherapy neurosurgery, I am not speaking metaphorically. We now have solid scientific evidence to suggest that the so-called "talking cure," originally devised by Freud, literally alters the way in which the neurons in the brain are connected to one another. This rewiring leads to changes in how you process, integrate, experience, and understand information and emotion. Recent scientific findings in neurobiology, cognitive science, developmental psychology, and psychotherapy research have made it possible for me, as a modern psychoanalyst, to do something Freud could only dream of: I can cast some of Freud's most fundamental psychological ideas in biological terms.

In this book I present evidence that shows how psychotherapy literally changes the structure of your brain. It actually can alter the web of interconnecting neural cells found in the gray matter of the cerebral cortex. Taken together over time, these physical changes in how neurons are connected help us to produce new internal representations of self and other, changing the ingrained neural patterns about relationships that were laid down during early childhood development. The techniques of psychodynamic psychotherapy—from the use of free association and the exploration of dreams to the probing of the evolving patient-therapist relationship itself—make sense in neuronal terms. I believe that the new evidence explains how and why the "talking cure" works at the cellular level. I hope to put the neuron back into neurosis.

A century ago, Freud—a neurologist by training and a biologist in his soul—had as his goal the integration of the psychological and the biological, when he set out on his ambitious *Project for a Scientific Psychology* in 1895. He soon concluded that not enough was known about the workings of the brain to permit such a synthesis, and he was forced to put his pet project on the back burner. Now, one hundred years after he gave up on it, prospects for a scientific psychology are heating up again as we begin to conceptualize how psychotherapy changes the brain.

Do not misunderstand my attempts to integrate Freud's techniques with recent research findings as a defense of all his ideas. Some of them—his views on female development, for example—are culture-bound and outmoded. Freud was a product of his time, just like the rest of us. But he was also a genius, with a prescient view of psychotherapy. Many of his discoveries make better sense today because of what we have learned about the brain. Much of this book describes what Freud couldn't possibly have known one hundred years ago. It should give you new respect for how much Freud did manage to understand about the mind. Now let's return to my microsurgery with Katie to see how we are working together to rearrange her mind by exploring and reshaping her brain.

A bull in a china shop. What are the origins of this expression? I contemplate the masculinity of the bull, and wonder: Did Katie's mother see her athletic daughter's vim and vigor as somehow masculine and threatening? But this question will have to wait as Katie careens off in another direction, remembering a story that involves real shattering glass.

"I don't think I've told you this, but as a toddler I broke the last of three milk glass dishes that my mother had on the coffee table. I think they were some of the few household trinkets my mother and father could afford at that point in their marriage, and my mother was particularly attached to them. I broke them in order, first the largest, then the middle-sized one, and finally only the smallest one was left. Mom later told me that when I broke the last one, she practically threw me across the room and into my crib. I think she must have felt really guilty about it afterwards. The story seems vaguely familiar to me, though I don't know now if I actually remember it or if it seems familiar from baby pictures."

"How does it show up in baby pictures?" I ask, puzzled.

"Well, there's one of me at about eighteen months, fingering the last of the three glass bowls a little while before I broke it. It was heart-shaped and white with tiny round balls around the edges, like little pearls."

I am asking myself why, if her mother didn't want Katie to break it, there is a photograph of this event, why Katie was allowed to play with the dish, even captured doing so in the photo as if it were cute. After all, if you lead a bull into a china shop, the results are predictable.

As she tells me the first story, Katie is reminded of another glass story. In this second tale, a three-year-old Katie slips away from her parents' cocktail party, climbs up on her bed, and snags a glass jar of petroleum jelly sitting on her dresser. The jar slips to the floor and shatters, and Katie is found sitting on the floor, surrounded by broken glass, gamely chomping on a large piece. A party guest holds Katie upside down and shakes her, attempting to dislodge any pieces of glass caught in her mouth or throat. In the family lore, it is an episode that captures Katie's adventurous spirit and natural curiosity, yet hints that these qualities are potentially dangerous, even deadly.

After hearing this second story, I decide it's time to try to tie together these themes of fragile relationships, natural curiosity, and shattering glass. "We've discussed how your adventurousness and curiosity and maybe even your competence threatened to disrupt your relationship with your mother by making you not need her. She needed you to need her, and if you didn't, she would feel angry and hurt. It's as if the relationship itself, the bond between you and your mother, was fragile and easy to shatter. And now, you're going off on your own, without me," I remind Katie, "on a big business trip that is the direct result of your effective efforts at work. I think you're concerned about whether *I* can tolerate your capability and your independence. I think you're concerned that one or both of us—or maybe our relationship— will get hurt the way I am hurt in the dream."

I feel certain that my interpretation has literally touched a nerve when Katie begins to cry. "In a way I feel like I've spent my whole life trying to make up for hurting my mother by leaving her. Maybe part of holding myself back at work is that I want to be sure I'm not too competent and don't leave her too far behind. I guess it's possible that I'm also worried that I'll hurt you, too, even though I get the sense that you're stronger, you don't need me to need you."

"I think you're very worried that you can't be competent and independent and also remain close and connected to your mother and to me as well."

"It's funny because when I was coming here today, I was tempted to buy flowers for you," Katie says, "maybe as a kind of going-away present, a way to be sure you're not really angry or hurt while I'm gone. I guess to let you know that I love you and need you even though I'm going off on my own for a while."

"We do need to stop here for today," I say, rising from my chair to open the door for Katie. "I hope you have a good trip." "Thanks," she says shyly, looking down at my hand as I go to open the door. I extend my hand and she pauses, looking me in the eye for a moment. Then we shake hands.

Soon after he set aside his *Project for a Scientific Psychology*, Freud turned to his first major work, *The Interpretation of Dreams*, calling dreams the "royal road" to the unconscious. This misunderstood and often-parodied aspect of Freudian treatment remains an integral aspect of psychodynamic therapy today. I believe dreams form an important route into the contents of the networks of neurons that comprise the cerebral cortex. Freud's theory of how dreams arise is largely unsupported by modern, brain-based dream research, but dreams continue to provide psychotherapy with fertile ground for exploration and change.

We now know that dreams occur primarily during periods of sleep known as rapid eye movement (REM) sleep. Such sleep generally begins about ninety minutes after we fall asleep, and occurs at regular intervals about four times nightly, giving us ample opportunity to catch a dream for later analysis despite the fact that the functioning of the brain during sleep makes dreams hard to remember.

Dream researcher J. Allan Hobson, in his fascinating book *The Dreaming Brain*, describes the dreaming process in terms of what he calls the "activation-synthesis hypothesis." According to this theory, REM sleep occurs when a group of neurons located deep in the brain, in an area called the brainstem, become active and begin to fire rapidly. These cells, called reticular formation neurons, slowly come to life because nearby cells responsible for awakeness gradually cease their firing. The awakeness cells normally inhibit or suppress the reticular formation neurons, so as they fade, activity in the reticular formation neurons emerges and becomes predominant.

The reticular formation neurons seem to do three main things. First, they actively inhibit incoming sensory information from the world, eliminating our usual channels of information about what we see, hear, touch, and smell. Like an angry child who puts his hands over his ears and shouts loudly to avoid hearing a parent scold him, the reticular neurons scream at external reality, blocking all or almost all sensory input to the higher areas of the brain where it is usually processed. In Katie's case, little or none of what is happening in the world around her as she lies sleeping affects her inner dream experience. We know, of course, that there are times when external information does in fact intrude on REM sleep—a ringing alarm clock may become an annoying telephone in a dream—but these events are the amusing exceptions to the rule.

The second task the activated reticular neurons perform is to blockade motor output, the normal pathways by which we move around in the world. These neurons send messages to the spinal cord motor neurons that cause the paralysis of sleep, conveniently keeping us from acting out our dreams. When we dream, the usual neurons in our motor cortex that make us able to move around during the day are actually given commands to fire, but when they reach the spinal cord, these orders are rescinded. Katie does not move, she does not act out her dream by getting out of bed and attempting to leave the room. There is some evidence in the dream itself that she is somewhat aware of this paralysis. She cannot stop the falling glass tabletop because it feels as if she cannot move!

The reticular formation neurons also activate the cerebral cortex, the thin gray layer of brain tissue that comprises the surface of the brain. The neurons send volleys of stimulation known as PGO waves, (short for pontine-geniculate-occipital, the three ascending areas of the brain in which the waves occur). These volleys originate in the pons, a lower-brain area that coordinates head and eye movements, causing the rapid side-to-side eye movements typical of the dreaming state, then progress upward to the geniculate nucleus, a sensory relay station, then on to the occipital cortex, the site of vision. Stimulation of the occipital cortex produces the vivid visual hallucinatory experiences of dreams. And stimulation of the occipital cortex also ultimately leads to activation of the association cortex, that area of the brain most responsible for synthesizing input from various sensory channels and combining it with stored past experiences—memories. Along the way to the association cortex, PGO waves also activate the limbic system, the area of the brain that is most responsible for the generation of emotion. Heightened firing in the limbic system, combined with feedback to the brain that tells it that the heartbeat and breathing have quickened, is probably the reason why we often have such strong emotions, such as fear, in our dreams.

Interestingly enough, the pattern of neural activity in the cerebral cortex during REM sleep is about equal in intensity to the activity of our cortexes when we are awake and thinking, reading, or talking. Our cortex is not "sleeping" at all. Disconnected from its usual sensory inputs and motor outputs, the brain in REM mode is nevertheless running, like an idling car in neutral, fueled by the random PGO waves that activate our higher cortex.

In waking life we do not have PGO waves, because our wakefulness neurons are firing and thereby suppressing the reticular formation neurons responsible for REM sleep. And in waking life, external sights and sounds bombard us, making it virtually impossible for us to focus solely on our internal stimuli alone. While some people are better daydreamers than others, most of us come back to reality as soon as someone calls our name. And when we are awake our movements are also constrained by what is physically possible, given our bodies and the laws of physics. In waking life we cannot fly by spreading our arms, and we cannot jump suddenly from one place to another. In contrast, in dreams we are limited only by what our brains, stimulated by random PGO wave firing, can dream up. Dreams make it possible, often in a refreshing way, to escape from the usual constraints of reality that keep us earthbound, boringly oriented in time and space.

But if dreams are such flights of fancy, why do they seem so real? Hobson proposes that they seem real to us because the PGO waves activate and stimulate the very same cortical areas that we use in waking life for perceiving and experiencing, thinking and feeling. When Katie's visual cortex is stimulated by a certain randomly occurring PGO wave, she may "see" a glass table. This is probably because the pattern of activity produced by a particular PGO wave closely resembles the pattern Katie's networks of neurons would produce if she saw a real table while awake. If the same pattern of activity is produced in a given network of nerve cells by a PGO wave as by really seeing a table, we will believe we are seeing a table. To the visual cortex, an input is an input, no matter whether it is internally or externally generated. And an input is "real" until proven otherwise.

The neurobiology of dreaming suggests that the intricate stories and intensely felt emotions of our dreams are directly related to what our brains are doing in REM sleep. Dream researchers like Hobson have argued that random cortical stimulation explains the non-sense of our dreams, the bizarre distortions of people, time, and place, and the often incongruous plots. No sooner has one part of the brain been activated than PGO waves are activating another part. An internal barrage of randomly occurring images and sensations is the result.

But more fascinating than the non-sense of dreams is the fact that much of the time our dreams do make sense, forming stories that enthrall us, narratives that seem packed with personal symbols and psychological meanings. How does the brain convert a kaleidoscopic barrage of randomly generated images and sensations into a cohesive and repetitive personal narrative? Why do our dreams make any sense at all? The answer to this question is at the heart of both how psychotherapy works and why dreams are useful stories to explore, providing what I would call a royal road to your neural netscapes.

When Katie returns from her trip, she tells me with excitement that she bought a ceramic figurine for her mother. "I got it right at the beginning of the trip and carried it all around with me. In fact, I was running a little late to my presentation because I was waiting for it to be properly boxed. I made it on time, but it was close."

"What's the figurine like?" I ask.

"It's a peasant woman with a duckling at her feet. She's feeding it, and the duck's head is angled upwards. After I bought it I realized that I should have gotten it at the end of the trip so I wouldn't have to worry about it getting broken. The duck's beak is really fragile. I carried it around very carefully and got it back in one piece, but I worried about it the whole trip. My mother loved it, but I still felt really guilty that she hasn't ever been to Europe and I have. No statue could make up for that." Katie looks guilty and begins to cry.

I try to bring her back to our last session. "Getting the figurine at the beginning of the trip sounds like a way of carrying your fragile relationship with your mother, and perhaps your easily shattered mother herself, around with you while you were gone. It sounds like buying the figurine caused you to attend all the while to the dangerousness of the trip and fragility of the figurine. And it almost made you late for that important presentation."

There it is again, that theme of fragile figures, tenuous connections, shattering glass.

While neuroscientists have been busy studying the neurobiology of the dreaming brain, psychotherapy researchers have been examining narratives told during psychotherapy, including the stories of dreams. Freud himself suggested the idea of "stereotype plates"—patterns based on our early experiences, indelibly etched upon our brains, that we carry around in our heads and repeatedly invoke as models when we interact with others. These "transference templates" have made sense to psychoanalytically oriented clinicians for years, but it was not until Lester Luborsky and his colleagues at the University of Pennsylvania developed a method for studying stories that the robustness of the concept became clear. They collected stories from a wide variety of settings. They asked people to make up stories, to tell stories from the past, and to recall their favorite childhood stories. They searched transcripts of psychotherapy sessions for narratives, including the stories of dreams.

The researchers then examined each person's array of stories, looking at the protagonist's wishes and fears, other characters' reactions to him or her, and his or her subsequent thoughts, feelings, and actions. What they found was astonishing. The patterns of each individual's stories were incredibly similar, whether the stories were made up or real, from childhood or the present, about the therapist or others. In terms of how we construct the central story of our lives, we may indeed have "one-track" minds. The stories were so much about conflicts in relationships, and their themes were so repetitive within a given person's collection, that the researchers termed their method the Core Conflictual Relationship Theme method.

Even more remarkable, when researchers studied what happened to these narratives over time, they found that the main story pattern became less pervasive as patients progressed in psychotherapy. The stories patients told later in therapy were less stereotyped and less rigidly adherent to the same core patterns than were the ones told earlier (if the treatment was progressing well). These changes in the story patterns were actually correlated with such indicators of improvement as reduction in depressive and anxiety symptoms.

Interestingly, a patient's *wishes* do not change significantly with treatment. Our wishes and fears are the built-in motivators, the engines that drive our stories as well as our pursuit of particular kinds of relationships. But the ways others respond to our wishes and fears and the ways we respond to others do change as the result of successful psychotherapy.

Researchers even have shown that patients did better when their therapists' comments more closely reflected the patients' predominant story patterns; therapists who were able to focus and remain focused on these core patterns achieved the most successful overall therapeutic outcomes. And patients who showed more understanding of their own story lines had more successful outcomes. These results suggest that our core stories are not only descriptive of our patterns but also keys to changing them.

Katie has now told me four stories about glass over the course of her analysis. Two were the stories in which she actually did break glass during her childhood. Another was the tale of the fragile yet ultimately unbroken figurine from her business trip. And the fourth was the shattering glass tabletop image that appeared in her dream. They all have a common story, a pattern that both she and I have come to recognize and articulate. Katie wants to feel self-assertive and independent and to go places, yet remain close to and accepted by me and by her mother as she strikes out on her own. She fears that her actions will inadvertently do something that injures us, shatters her relationships with us. She imagines we will react to her separation and independence by being literally and figuratively wounded, hurt, and angry. She reacts to this possibility by feeling sad, guilty, and anxious herself.

The actual historical event of Katie breaking her mother's last milk glass bowl as a toddler most closely parallels her dream narrative; she does accidentally break something, jeopardizing, at least temporarily, her relationship with her mother, who angrily throws her into her crib. The tales of Katie eating the glass and presenting her mother with the fig-

PREPARING FOR A MORTGAGE LOAN APPLICATION

Thank you for considering Educational Employees Credit Union for your financial needs.

At EECU, our goal is to work with you to find a mortgage loan that best meets your needs, and that's why we offer several types of loans. To help find the loan that is best for you, please complete the "Fast Start Real Estate Loan Inquiry" form. Then, visit our website or call us to review available loan options.

Once you've determined the type of mortgage loan you want, you can apply online anytime at www.myEECU.org. You can also apply by phone from 9 a.m. to 5 p.m., Monday through Friday at (800) 538-EECU or 559-437-7700 - select the Loan option followed by the Real Estate option.

You may want to start gathering the items listed on the reverse side. These documents may help you complete the loan application and may be required to process your loan.

EECU Mortgage Center
455 East Barstow Avenue, Fresno, CA 93710
(located on the west side of the Barstow Branch)
Fax: 559-225-0234

in Neurosis

the other two stories:
on her own, and her
h to become more in-
nnected to her mother

chaotic cacophony of
with its random PGO
ably similar stories of
oposed answer to this
is book. I believe that
hesizer," whose job it
racters for the unique
esizer is stimulated by
f REM sleep, the ac-
crank out a dream that
tains. The story syn-
monkey can play only
requests.
ue that the story syn-
rtex of the brain, with
areas responsible for
am suggesting that a
cortex functions as a
shapes our approach
s associative network
sleep, the resulting
es around which the
the synthesizer con-

tains representations of ourselves and others, building blocks with which we assemble our unique but characteristic construction of the story of our life.

I also propose that the biological connections between the neurons that make up the story synthesizer are literally strengthened or forged, weakened or broken—ultimately rewired—through the process of psychotherapy. When such rewiring occurs on a grand scale, through repeated experience and work on specific patterns, particular parts of the brain are permanently altered. Psychotherapy helps our monkey learn some new tunes.

There is exciting new convergent evidence from disparate fields of scientific inquiry that suggests that my theory is correct. Recent findings in cognitive science indicate that such a story synthesizer could arise from a network of relatively simple, interconnected neurons. Neurobiological findings show that the interconnections between neurons actually do change in response to experience, providing a glimpse of the cellular mechanism that underlies human learning, including learning in psychotherapy. Research on infant development is beginning to shed light on how the brain forms representations of self and other during childhood, in the process showing us how these representations arise naturally from our perceptual experiences in infancy. And we are beginning to understand how these early life experiences in turn shape the circuits in our brains that we use to regulate our emotions for the rest of our lives.

Katie came to therapy unaware that she even had a story synthesizer, let alone that it kept grinding out the same tale in situation after situation, relationship after relationship. If the story synthesizer in her cortex could speak for itself, it might say something like: "My choices are to be depressed, needy, and incapable (like my mother), yet connected to others, *or* to be competent and self-sufficient, yet all alone. My abilities, including my ability to be self-sufficient, are a constant threat to my fragile relationships with important others; in fact, these connections are so delicate that I can unintentionally shatter them without even knowing it until it is too late, harming myself and others in the process."

By the end of her therapy, what Katie's story synthesizer might say would be quite different. But the story synthesizer cannot speak for itself, at least not directly. So where in the process of psychotherapy, which sometimes seems so nebulous, can evidence for this change be found? Why not return to the realm of the dream, where the random firing of reticular neurons deep in the brain cranks up the story synthesizer in the neural networks on its surface? Like the panting of a couch potato in a high-impact aerobics class, dreams give away what shape the cortex is in.

Let's see what is different about Katie's dreams after a second year of psychotherapy.

I go to a large club, which, to my surprise, has a swimming pool. The sides of the pool are transparent; they allow you to see the legs of a person swimming underwater, to recognize who they are. I am surprised someone has spent the money to build a pool like this. I have heard it cost two million dollars to build. I notice a woman at one end, beckon-

*ing me into the water. I am a little frightened to jump in
and wonder if the pool will crack, but when I test the water
with a toe, it is warm. I get in and float comfortably on
my back.*

I am surprised, as I listen to this latest dream, to find myself thinking about the very beginning of my treatment with
Katie. When she first began psychotherapy, she felt concerned about whether or not she could actually be in therapy twice a week. Would she run out of things to say, her
verbalizations waning to a slow trickle? Would she be overwhelmed by feelings she had been warding off for years? She
compared beginning psychotherapy to diving into water that
was cold and uninviting, that took her breath away when she
entered it. She didn't know whether she would sink or swim.
Only when I reminded her that I was to be with her in the
water, swimming alongside, did she begin to be relieved. I
wondered if this dream, two years later, contained a possible
reference to our early interaction. This time the water into
which she dove was warm and welcoming. There is also a hint
of the image of glass in the transparent pool, which Katie feels
concerned might crack. This time it does not shatter, a tes-
timony, I believe, to the greater strength and resilience of
Katie's connections to me and to important other people in
her life.

Katie's own associations run along these lines as well, a
sign that we are on the same wavelength. She sees that this
time we are linked by our enjoyment of the warm water
rather than by the cold, hard, fragile glass that used to rep-

resent our bond. Meanwhile, Katie's relationships outside my office have gradually deepened as well. I hear things about her mother other than that she is fragile and dependent. When Katie returns from a weekend at home, her descriptions of her mother sound positively spunky, for the first time ever. One of the fascinating things about psychotherapy is that as the patient changes, the entire cast of characters her story synthesizer has encoded begins to shift as well.

As Katie's dream suggests, such personal change does not come cheap. (It seems to cost two million dollars!) However, change does come, and with it come signs of progress in Katie's life outside my office. She has had two rapid promotions and numerous successful presentations. She feels more in touch with and appreciative of her inner life. And in this second year, an important subplot of her central story has emerged. We now understand that Katie is not just afraid of accidentally hurting others, shattering her relationships with them. Some part of her actually *wants* to shatter them—especially if, like her relationship with her mother, they threaten to keep her unnecessarily tied to certain persons. She now sees that she is angry at those around her who need her to need them. And now that she knows that part of her wants to shatter them, the relationships she forms with others actually have become more resilient. Katie now knows she has conflicting feelings about how close and connected to be. In the context of an emotionally intense relationship with me, Katie's sense that relationships are tenuous has diminished. And as she feels safer with me, it becomes easier for her to experience the anger that she was spending psychic time and energy avoiding. During the two years of our work together, Katie and I have created a new narrative about who she is and how she came to be that way. I believe we have done so by carefully and systematically examining, challenging, and rewiring the story synthesizer her cortex contains.

When I work with dreams, I sometimes find myself wishing I could talk to Freud, because he was such a talented observer of human nature and its vicissitudes. As I get to know him better, I have more and more appreciation for the techniques he discovered and for the power his method provides in my day-to-day work with patients. But I wouldn't want a conversation with him to end in admiration only, with me seated at his knee gathering pearls of wisdom. I'd have some theoretical bones to pick with him, and I'd like to bring him up to date on the century's work in our field. For starters, I imagine he'd be impressed to hear that there are more people in psychoanalysis worldwide than ever before. I wonder what he'd think about Prozac, which has rescued so many from what he regarded as "normal" human misery. Given some of his views of the world, I'd tuck some free samples in his pocket and gently suggest that perhaps he should try it. But mostly I'd try to tempt him with some juicy scientific morsels, some details about the neurobiology of sea slugs, perhaps. I imagine he'd be hungry after all these years, yearning for a taste of biology, seeking food for thought. But where to take Freud after all these years? Sushi? Pacific Rim? Continental? As I think about the options, I realize that if I really want to bring him up to date, I should take him to Star-bucks for—what else?—Viennese coffee. And I'd fill him in on how things are turning out in this Decade of the Brain: things he couldn't have known—but of which he might have dreamed.

2

In Search of the
Cheshire Cat

By the way, I had a friend for dinner last night," says Alice, taking a small sip from the bottle of Poland Spring water she has brought to the session. She always brings the bottle to sessions, never drinking much of it and never discarding it in the wastebasket on her way out the door.

Both Alice and I believe that inviting her friend over is an incremental, positive step along the pathway to changing her mind. She came to treatment quite depressed and demoralized, in the process of writing her dissertation. She soon responded to an antidepressant, but after she was feeling better it became clear to both of us that there were issues about relationships that medication couldn't touch. She began twice-weekly therapy to try to change the theme her story synthesizer kept cranking out in relationship after relationship.

The Talking Cure

There were two stories that Alice strongly related to that she had told me early in her psychotherapy by way of describing how she felt. The first was a Sufi tale about a man who lived on a mountain above a town. The gods told him that he should save water because the rainwater that fell after a certain time would not be fit to drink. He saved water and drank his safe supply on the mountain, watching the people in the town below. Ignorant of the gods' plan, the townspeople drank the nonpotable water and became crazy, dancing and singing. They were insane, but happy and together, while the man who watched from on high was sane, but sad and alone. Interpreted through the lens of this story, the fact that Alice invited her friend for dinner could be understood as a figurative journey halfway down the mountain, out of her hermit's lair. But which water was she sipping in the session?

The second story emerged more gradually. I nicknamed this story, an amalgam of *Alice in Wonderland* and *Peter Pan*, "Alice in Neverland." Alice had felt especially drawn to both these stories as a child, perhaps in part because she shared a name with one of the tales' protagonists. But the appeal of the two stories and the unique way she had combined their themes went far deeper than that.

Alice in Wonderland tells of Alice's adventures among the fantastic and sometimes spooky creatures who exist in a whole other world down the Rabbit Hole. The White Rabbit, late for an important date, consults his pocket watch as he scurries to and fro. The self-satisfied Cheshire Cat appears then disappears, "beginning with the end of the tail, and ending with the grin, which remained some time after the rest of it had gone." The Queen of Hearts bosses everyone around, screaming "off with their heads" with little provocation as she rushes around the croquet field strewn with hedgehogs and flamingos. Strange potions appear with instructions to "Drink me." And when Alice does, the potions make her bigger, smaller, taller, shorter, playing in a scary way with reality.

As for *Peter Pan*, Alice could quote the opening passage by heart, so often had she heard the story as a child. "It begins with Wendy and her mother in the garden," Alice told me: " 'All children, except one, grow up. They soon know that they will grow up, and the way Wendy knew was this. One day when she was two years old she was playing in the garden, and she plucked another flower and ran with it to her mother. I suppose she must have looked rather delightful, for Mrs. Darling put her hand to her heart and cried, "Oh, why can't you remain like this for ever!" This was all that passed between them on the subject, but henceforth Wendy knew that she must grow up. You always know after you are two. Two is the beginning of the end.' "

I speculated to myself that the fact that Alice's mother read her the tale so often suggested that it might have important meanings for her as well; and in fact Alice recollected that her mother always got tearful while reading this first paragraph.

Alice seemed to have combined the Sufi story and Alice in Neverland into the story of her early life. She took the symbols of drinking and craziness from each, and made certain conclusions: sharing water with others can be crazy-making;

drinking can play around with your reality, changing your size but never making you grow up. This link between drinking and crazy unpredictability made the question that had been nagging at me in recent sessions all the more urgent: Was the ubiquitous water bottle freshly purchased, or had Alice refilled her water bottle in my bathroom before the session? Could she be sharing my water? It might be a powerful indicator of trust, considering the crazy-making potential of drinking from the bottle in both the Sufi tale and in Alice in Neverland. How could I explain its significance to her managed care company? I imagined writing as a goal on her next treatment plan, "Patient will drink tap water at my office." Perhaps that would fly if Alice had obsessive-compulsive disorder and fears of contamination. Then drinking the water could be construed as a behavioral therapy intervention, in which she confronted something about which she was phobic. I knew Alice was indeed "phobic" about drinking the crazy-making water. But even though the act of drinking my tap water was itself concrete, the shift in symbolism it suggested was much more abstract; I suspected that if Alice refilled her water bottle at my office, it would herald a shift in her view of how dangerous drinking water with others could be.

I have argued that the random neuronal firings of REM sleep stimulate our cortex in chaotic ways, stirring up the network of neurons that contain our most central personal stories. But what is the evidence that this story synthesizer can be found in the cortex, and how might shifts in the interconnections of its neurons lead us to change our minds in fundamental ways? One hint about the answer to the first question came from the work of Wilder Penfield in the 1950s. Penfield, a Canadian neurosurgeon who founded the Montreal Neurological Institute, pioneered a unique surgical technique to eliminate epilepsy in patients with severe forms of it. His method was designed to localize and eradicate the abnormal areas of the brain, places with tiny scars that served to trigger the seizures. By excising these areas surgically, Penfield was able to free his severely impaired patients from seizures permanently. He developed a unique method for determining where these problematic areas of the brain actually were; he opened the skulls of his patients while they were awake, in order to expose and electrically stimulate the surfaces of their brains. This is less barbaric than it sounds, since the brain itself has no pain receptors and the patients received local anesthesia to block pain from the scalp and skull.

When Penfield stimulated the cerebral cortex, he saw snatches of the mind in action. In response to the electrical stimulation, patients sometimes recalled passages of music, interactions with friends and family, and even entire scenes with lavish detail from their childhoods. These were sometimes experienced with "movie-like" clarity. For example, Penfield wrote,

M. heard "a mother calling her little boy" when point 11 on the first temporal convolution was stimulated. When it was repeated at once, without warning she heard the

same thing. When it was repeated twice again at the same point, she heard it each time, and she recognized that she was near her childhood home. At point 12 nearby . . . stimulation caused her to hear a man's voice and a woman's voice "down along the river somewhere." And she saw the river. It was a place "I was visiting," she said, "when I was a child." Three minutes later, while the electrode was held in place at 13 she exclaimed that she heard voices late at night and that she saw the "big wagons they used to haul the animals (of a circus) in."

Penfield recognized that when he probed the brains of his patients, causing their interconnected networks of neurons to fire, he was somehow bringing aspects of their unique personal experiences—including the emotions that accompanied them—"to mind."

Evidence that the cerebral cortex is the seat of the mind can be found also by examining what happens to the brain in various dementing illnesses, such as Alzheimer's disease, that cause people to "lose their minds." When you look under a microscope at the brain of someone with Alzheimer's disease, you see that the cerebral cortex contains plaques and tangles that ruin the normal neural architecture; they are like pits from mortar shells on a facade that is otherwise magnificently constructed. As their names suggest, brain plaques and tangles—areas in which there are abnormal globs of protein filaments and other deposits—are bad news for cortical function. As these lesions affect more and more little areas of the cortex, patients gradually lose their sense of themselves and of their significant others as the individual sets of memories and ideas they have formed over a lifetime are eroded. Alzheimer's disease provides sad but compelling evidence that the seat of the mind is the cerebral cortex.

Another reason to believe that the cerebral cortex is the seat of the mind is that there are not that many other parts of the brain that are contenders—available to house the mind. The structure of the brain itself suggests that the "mind"— by which I mean that collection of thoughts, feelings, memories and experiences of the world that makes each person unique—is located in the cerebral cortex. Other parts of the brain are assigned other important tasks, and these tasks are not only specialized but also common to all of us, like seeing and breathing and controlling the movements of our limbs as we navigate in the world. These lower regions of the cortex are highly specialized, wired to work in the same particular way in all of us. For instance, the specialized visual cells in my retina connect in essentially the same way as yours do to lower brain areas on their way to the occipital cortex, where visual representations of the outer world are constructed. When inputs reach this visual cortex, they are processed similarly in different people.

The situation changes when this input moves beyond the primary visual cortex and on to the association cortex. There, the input stimulates memories and is integrated with past experience as well as stimuli from other modalities. In addition, the limbic system, which is a highly interconnected area used for short-term memory and the representation of emotion, is stirred up by the incoming visual information. Together, the association and limbic cortical systems contain the records of all of our unique experiences and feelings.

Suppose you and I both see the White Rabbit from *Alice's Adventures in Wonderland*. Our retinal cells transmit various pieces of information about the shape, texture, color, and movement of the White Rabbit to our cerebral cortex. We both recognize that the White Rabbit *is* a White Rabbit as this information is processed in our primary visual cortex. Until this point, the neural pathways that relay this information are fairly stereotyped, with little significant variation between individuals. We both know a White Rabbit when our visual cortex sees one.

The incoming perception of the White Rabbit also causes ripples of brain activation in both the deeper, less-specialized limbic cortex and the higher-order association cortex. All sorts of wonderful individual associations now occur, complete with their emotional tones. The White Rabbit may make me think of the fun I had playing with my grandfather's rabbits as a child, while it reminds you of the Easter bunny. These thoughts bring other associated thoughts and feelings along with them. I may feel sad about my grandfather's death, then feel guilty that I haven't called my grandmother this week, while you recall your disappointment that year when your sister got a bigger chocolate egg. If you observe your own internal mental life, you will begin to recognize this characteristic flow: perceptions stirring up associated ideas and feelings to form the web of interlinking ideas, affects, and memories that make up your mind.

What does this higher-order association cortex, the site of the mind, look like? The cerebral cortex is made up primarily of pyramidal cells, neurons that appear to be quite flexible and multipurpose in nature, like CD-ROMs, which store text, images, music, movies, and games side by side. The information the networks contain, though, is stored not on a static physical entity like a plastic disk, but in the living and changing interconnections among the pyramidal cells themselves. The association cortex is a flexible storage system contained in a network of interconnected cells that can change as we grow and learn, forming our own special sets of neural connections.

We can now do more than speculate that the association cortex, with its limbic-system connections, is the seat of the mind. In a recent study by Nancy Andreasen and her colleagues at the University of Iowa, researchers used PET scans to study the brain functions of patients who were free-associating. PET, or positron emission tomography, shows which areas of the brain are functioning in high gear. Patients are given an injection of a radioactive substance (known as a tracer), which concentrates in those areas of the brain where blood flow is highest, yielding a picture of the brain in action. When patients free-associated while being PET-scanned, their higher brain areas, the association cortex, clearly were most active. This study provided evidence for the idea that the story synthesizer, which brings order and narrative coherence to the random activations of our neurons during REM sleep, is spread out within a weblike system of interconnected nerve cells in this uppermost, thin gray layer of brain.

But how could a network of interconnected pyramidal cells store interlinking ideas? How might these cells contain memories? One answer to this question that was fashionable in the era of brain localization at the beginning of this century was the one neuron–one idea theory. In this model, one neuron would stand for one idea, such as your grandmother. This idea fell out of favor when Karl Lashley removed more and more small units of the cortex, which he termed engrams, from dogs. He demonstrated that the dogs functioned well, with no noteworthy gaps in their memory and behavior, until a critical amount of brain tissue was removed. After this point, the dogs performed poorly on every kind of memory test. Such results would not make sense if particular cells stored certain ideas or representations. If Lashley removed your grandmother neuron, you should forget your grandmother. But this is not what happens.

Lashley's findings suggest that memories and representations of people and things are distributed rather than localized. In other words, rather than having a single neuron or set of local neurons represent your grandmother, memories of your grandmother are contained in webs of interlinking neurons distributed in the cortex. This idea makes good computational sense as well. Although 10 billion neurons seems like an impressively large hard drive, if you need one neuron for each byte of information you store, over a lifetime you could find yourself in the position of a 40 megabyte hard drive in a Windows 95 world: suffering from information overload. If ideas and memories are stored instead as patterns of activation across many neurons, a network of neurons, your computational power would be many times higher than in the model of one memory, one neuron. Put simply, a network of neurons can comfortably store many memories, not just one per neuron. Although every pyramidal cortical neuron is certainly not connected to the other 10 billion, pyramidal cells do form extensive networks with one another. You can begin to get a sense of what a flexible yet powerful computational system the pyramidal networks could comprise.

I want to know, so I ask: "Did you fill your water bottle from my tap today before the session?"

"Yes," says Alice, somewhat surprised by my question.

"I'm wondering if that doesn't mean you think of my water as less scary, dangerous, and crazy-making. After all, you used to bring water from home to our meetings."

"Well, I think that's a little far-fetched, Herr Doktor," Alice asserts in her best Viennese accent. I grow quiet, waiting to see what will happen next. I think about Alice's parents, who are alcoholics. They are not the angry, screaming monsters that I hear about so often in the stories of children raised by alcoholic parents. Instead, Alice's parents drank and then became rather numb, sitting around the living room together in front of the buzzing TV set until they fell asleep in a drunken stupor.

Alice's parents seemed to be trying to drown their despair over the death of Alice's two-year-old brother when Alice was one. Amazingly enough, her parents did not tell Alice until she was in high school that she had ever had an older brother at all. They did not talk or perhaps even think about him when they were sober. I thought about Alice's family in terms of the themes we had been developing, and I wondered: Was drinking a gateway to a hidden world for Alice's parents, one in which they could remember her brother while protected by the mind-numbing anesthetic effects of alcohol?

Alice's brother had died of a genetically transmitted disease that made him unable to digest certain forms of sugar that are present in many different foods. One day Alice, who had just begun to crawl, shared her juice bottle with the already-retarded Max; drinking the juice could make him worse because it contained sugars he couldn't digest. The episode was important: it was Alice's growing up, bringing with it her greater capacity to interact with Max, that led her parents to decide to put Max in a home for the retarded, in which he soon died at about two.

The secretiveness with which her parents treated her brother's death was understandable; at the time Max was diagnosed, it was clear that his illness was genetically transmitted, but there was no test for it, no chance of finding out whether Alice might be a carrier or even have the illness herself. In order to tolerate having a second child, aware of the very real possibility that they could face a second death from the same horrible disease, Alice's parents, understandably, had wanted to block Max out of their minds.

Their silence, however, created a home environment in which nothing was quite as it seemed. For years Alice saw a small picture of a young boy on her mother's dresser, but she was told that the boy in the photo was a cousin. Alice thought the picture looked like her, but somehow she knew to keep this comment to herself. She presented this historical information early in therapy as if her parents had dealt with Max's death in a normal way—as if their secrecy was no big deal. But over time the secret had permeated everything, taking on even more importance because it was secret than because of Max's death. It helped to explain why Alice's parents sometimes reacted strangely, as when her mother cried uncontrollably at Alice's birthday parties, or her father insisted rather angrily that Alice play catch with him even though she hated it. And somehow neither parent seemed concerned that Alice's favorite character growing up was Ophelia. They did not protest when she hung above her bed a print of Ophelia, a suicide, floating down the river bedecked in flowers.

How might a network of interconnecting neurons give rise to the interlinking symbols and ideas we explore in psychotherapy? The "grandmother neuron" idea was appealing because it gave us a concrete way to think about where in the brain various ideas are housed. It is the ultimate in localization. Touch my grandmother neuron and you touch the spot in my brain that represents her. But as computer science and artificial intelligence models have become more advanced, scientists increasingly have come to appreciate the power of what they call parallel distributed processing. In parallel distributed processing, a network of interconnected neurons represents ideas or memories as a specific pattern of activation across the individual nerve cells.

When researchers working in the field of artificial intelligence attempted to model human capabilities such as memory, language, and learning on serial computers, they did not get very far. Your PC or MacIntosh is a serial computer that performs operations correctly because your software spells out the rules by which it conducts various tasks. Serial computers do each task in order, following the step-by-step rules laid down for them by the computer's central processing unit. A serial computer works like Betty Crocker making a cake from a box, beginning with "Combine cake mix with eggs," following the directions sequentially, in lockstep order, and ending with "Cool cake on a rack."

Researchers gradually came to realize that humans are not good at what computers are good at, and that computers are terrible at things humans do with ease. For instance, could you instantly tell whether a name you were looking for on a list was present in a list of 100,000 names? Your PC could. Could you quadruple a recipe in your head in fractions of a second? For your PC this would be a piece of cake. But there are things that you are better at. You could pick out the face of a friend in a sea of people quite readily; no computer designed so far could do this task as well or as quickly. Humans are particularly good at pattern recognition, while serial computers do well on tasks that involve adding, moving, and comparing data. As a psychoanalyst, I find this heartening, because I believe that psychotherapy itself is a form of complex pattern recognition. It is nice that my natural, biological computational skills dovetail with my pattern-recognition task!

Human brains are hooked up as networks of neurons that perform many tasks simultaneously, in parallel. In other words, rather than having one powerful master chef who knows all the steps to follow in order to make a cake, the parallel distributed processing cooking show involves a team of cooks, none of whom is expert like the master chef, but all of whom can do different tasks at the same time that ultimately lead to the production of a cake. The cook who makes the icing might do so at the same time as the cook who sifts the flour. The preparation is done in parallel steps that are distributed among the cooks. The knowledge of how to make the cake, like your knowledge about your grandmother, does not reside in a single location but is spread out among all the cells of the network.

Artificial intelligence (AI) researchers have created computer models of specific cognitive functions in hopes of learning more about how the brain actually operates. Since AI researchers have focused on developing computer models in which processing takes place in parallel, rather than sequential, steps, something amazing has happened. For the first time, researchers have created models known as neural network models, which are good at things people are good at: pattern recognition.

In such a model, various ideas are represented by different patterns of activation across a network of neurons. For example, a certain activation pattern of neurons causes me to think "Cheshire Cat." If I then allow my brain to move naturally from one idea to another, the activation pattern which produced the thought "Cheshire Cat" will stimulate a closely related pattern of activity, rather than some third idea whose pattern of activation is less similar. Thus, "Cheshire Cat" is more likely to flow into a thought of my pet when I was five than it is to remind me of a day at the beach (unless, of course,

Cheshire Cats	White Rabbits	Mock Turtles
Neurodes 1–16	Neurodes 1–16	Neurodes 1–16

	Versions		
1	+ - + + - + - + + + + - - - - +	+ - + + - - - - + - + - + + - -	+ + - + - + + - + - + + + + + +
2	+ - + + - + - + + + - - - - - +	+ - + + - - - - + + + - + + - -	+ + - + - - + - + - + + + + + +
3	+ - + + + + - + + + + - - - - +	+ + + + - - - - + - + - + + - -	+ + - + - + + - + + + + + + + +

Prototype		
+ - + + - - - + + + + - - - - +	+ - + + - - - - + - + - + + - -	+ + - + - + + - + - + + + + + +

Probe		
+ - + + +	+ + - - - - + - +	+ + - + - + +

Figure 1

I see the beach as a giant litter box). Since my life experiences are what lead me to connect ideas in particular ways, this free association reveals the links between the various contents of my mind.

How does this flow happen in the brain cells? In neural network models, the brain's memory of various patterns of activation is stored in the "weights," or strengths of interconnection, between the individual neurons. Learning occurs through changes in the strength of the connections between various neurons.

The "auto-associator" computer model, developed by cognitive scientists David Rummelhart and James McClelland and their colleagues, provides an illustration of this process. In this model there are sixteen simple processing units with properties like neurons in the brain. These units are called "neurodes" in cognitive science, a term that stresses their similarity to neurons. All each neurode knows how to do is to add up the amount of input it receives from other neurodes and to fire or not fire, depending on whether the total input is greater than its activation threshold or not. In the auto-associator network, all the neurodes start out in a zero position, with no strong negative or positive connections between them.

Now suppose that we present the sixteen-neurode network with three different versions of Cheshire Cats, three different versions of White Rabbits, and three different versions of Mock Turtles. Each presentation yields a particular pattern of activation across the sixteen neurodes. For example, suppose the input of the first version of a Cheshire Cat produces the particular pattern of activation shown in Figure 1. Neurode 1 is *on*, or *activated*, (+); neurode 2 is *off*, or *inactivated*, (-); neurodes 3 and 4 are on, neurode 5 is off, and so forth, across the sixteen neurodes.

The general rule for this process is: "Neurodes that fire together, wire together." For example, in the first presentation of the Cheshire Cat, the neurodes that fired together, neurodes 1, 3, and 4, become more strongly connected to one another. In contrast, those that did not fire together, neurodes 1 and 2, remain neutral. Each presentation, then, with its particular pattern of activation, leads to changes in how the six-teen neurodes are connected.

As our network is presented with version after version of various cats, rabbits, and turtles, the specific patterns of activation that occur lead to specific alterations in the strengths of the connections between the various neurodes.

After showing our sixteen-neurode network all our versions of Cheshire Cats, White Rabbits, and Mock Turtles in any order we wish, we end up with sixteen neurodes that have various connection strengths between them. These connections reflect the "learning" of our sixteen neurodes about the different examples we have presented. We can now ask it questions to see what it has actually learned. We can ask it to give us a description of a prototypic Cheshire Cat, and it can do so, by pulling out the commonalities among the examples of cats it has seen. The extraction of this Average Cheshire Cat arises quite naturally from the fact that the three cat examples the network has seen have various features in common.

If we next feed a specific pattern of activation to the network without indicating whether it is a cat, a rabbit, or a turtle, our network will be able to decide which category it fits the best. The specific examples the network has learned, and the generation of prototypes resulting from this learning, are remarkably robust. We can give our network a fragment of a pattern, say, just the tail of the Cheshire Cat, and the network still can determine that we are referring to a cat, not a turtle or rabbit. The network can be given even faulty clues, say, a fragment of a pattern where some neurodes are incorrectly turned on or off, and still it will settle into the best-fitting pattern of activation. For example, if the network is given the fragmented and incorrect probes shown in Figure 1, it still can decide which fragments are most consistent with cats, rabbits, or turtles.

All these features of our sixteen-neurode network are quite consistent with how human memory and cognition actually work. Although we provided our network with no specific instructions about exactly what to learn, it has created a flexible information-storage system. This self-organizing property is essential for humans, since during much of life we are not told what to learn, not cued about what we will be tested on. Our network can spontaneously generalize, give us a prototype based on the examples it has seen. Notice that we never told the auto-associator network the special properties of Cheshire Cats. We just showed it some examples and it extracted the common features on its own.

Humans are good, sometimes too good, at generalizing spontaneously about things they know little about, using their past experiences as guides. Suppose we learn that a Cheshire Cat has moved into the neighborhood. If we have formed a prototype of Cheshire Cats that suggests that they are lazy and cannot be trusted, then we are likely to see our new neighbor incorrectly in this light. Our capacity for generalization can be misused easily in a way that promotes stereotyping and presumption. Yet our capacity to generalize also can allow us to draw accurate conclusions that are useful as well. If Cheshire Cats eat chocolate cake and chocolate ice cream, they probably like chocolate doughnuts, too.

Our sixteen-neurode model also is good at retrieving a

whole representation from a partial description, just as we are. If someone asks us (or our neurode network) "What's that *Alice in Wonderland* character who's always in a hurry?" we know they mean the White Rabbit. We use minimal clues to elicit information from others all the time in daily life:

"What's the name of that girl? You know, the one who you went to high school with? I think she used to be a singer."

"I don't know who you mean."

"Sure, you know, we saw her at the mall that time when you bought that gold silk blouse. In the parking lot."

"Oh, you mean Alice. You know, I should give her a call. She's been keeping to herself lately."

Humans and neural networks are good at retrieving correct information even in the face of erroneous clues, when part of the information given is wrong. Thus, if our friend says we knew Alice from camp and we actually knew her from high school, we probably still would be able to figure out who she means. The fact that one piece of the information was off would not derail our recollection efforts. This robustness of our associative memory in the face of incorrect information is called graceful degradation, and it is a little like aging gracefully. As we get less and less precise information to work with (or celebrate more and more birthdays), we ultimately do less and less well. But we often do better than expected; we can perform successfully even when conditions are not ideal.

You may be losing patience with neural networks or, perhaps more accurately, with me at this point, wondering what they have to do with Alice's therapy. My point is that they suggest that we are designed to manufacture connections between things, to associate one thing with another. We automatically find a way to make sense of the world around us even when the connections we have formed are wrong. Thus, Alice as a child might associate her mother crying at her birthday party and crying at the first paragraph of *Peter Pan* with her own growing up. And in one sense her neural networks would be right. But her networks are missing a key piece of information: the existence of Max. Still, Alice does her best, using Alice in Neverland and the man on the mountain to synthesize her experiences into a cohesive whole.

So what happens once Alice's parents tell her about Max, when she is in high school, and this knowledge is added into the mix of interconnected events and ideas? This missing piece of information is the psychological key to unlocking the meaning of her mother's tears at the opening of *Peter Pan* or at Alice's birthday party. If Alice had understood this association earlier, her networks might have been organized in a different fashion, with a place for her brother and with associations between his death and her mother's sadness while Alice was growing up.

But Alice's networks, with their built-in associations, have been organized since early childhood in the absence of this information. Once she learns about Max, it is too late for her to go back and reorganize all those interconnected themes on her own. Her networks already have evolved in a particular way. The new information gets stuck on to Alice's networks the way a wad of chewing gum is stuck to a theater seat.

The gum does not fundamentally change the structure of the chair itself.

Part of our task in psychotherapy is to reach into Alice's adult networks and disconnect those neurons that link growing up with sadness. This reexamination and reshaping of networks laid down in early life is probably the neurobiological equivalent of what analysts term "working through." While the need for reshaping is less clear and dramatic in patients whose families do not have such big secrets as Alice's, most adults have formed some false connections, some representations that made sense at the time but were erroneous and now are problematic. Alice's theory that her parents didn't want her to grow up organized and gave a cohesive meaning to their frightening and otherwise incomprehensible behavior at the time. Of course, Alice's parents were not the only ones who had conflicted feelings about Alice's growing up. Alice herself acknowledged that growing up would mean dealing with her sexuality, taking on new responsibilities, and caring for herself. But as an adult in her mid-thirties, Alice has reasons for wanting to grow up that outweigh her wish to remain a child. She is increasingly aware of things on which she is missing out.

To me, the notion of working through has always evoked the image of helping to "comb" the patient's neural networks into a more ruly configuration, unsnarling the parts that shouldn't be tangled up. The job requires not only patience but also the persistence to see it through. If we are too rough, trying to get the tangles out too rapidly, we risk hurting the patient, the psychic equivalent of pulling her hair. But if we are not persistently attentive to the places that seem the most in need of combing, we run the risk of never making a difference in disentangling the snarled core themes, the aberrant arrangements of neural connections. Of course, the best neural-network "do" is not necessarily the one with no tangles at all. Just as teasing gives hair lift and body, some conflict gives our lives richness. As an analyst, at times I feel like a good stylist, able to imagine what the neural networks might look like when we have reshaped them enough. Of course, as with a haircut, the style we choose ultimately is up to the patient. I am there to help her achieve the results she desires.

The psychoanalyst Heinz Kohut, who started the self psychology movement, called the mother's vision of what a child might become in later life a "gleam in the mother's eye." This gleam conveys a sense of potential, a feeling of being seen and understood, to the child. Like a good parent, I have to be able to love my patients as they are right now, envisioning futures full of possibilities for them, yet respecting the choices that they make. Although I have been envisioning Alice's descent down the mountain for some time, it is possible that after successful psychotherapy, she might choose to live there forever.

As Alice begins to socialize more, I find myself feeling inexplicably sad. I think back to the first pages of *Peter Pan* and know that they were important in terms of Alice's treatment, but I cannot remember them. It's funny, because I find I have no recollection of the details of the story of Peter Pan. I know vaguely that it is the story of a boy who never grows up, that Neverland is the place he retreats to, that the story involves a fight with Captain Hook, but I'm fuzzy about the rest. In fact, as a child, I never liked the story.

The sadness stays with me and grows as Alice blossoms. Then one weekend I find myself at the bookstore, browsing in the children's section. I come across *Peter Pan* without quite realizing that I was looking for it, and in an instant I am engrossed. As I reread the part where Mrs. Darling is sad because Wendy has to grow up, I remember Alice's recitation, and I think of her mother's tears. Am I feeling sad the way her mother might have? I read on and find myself at a point in the story that strikes me as apt.

> *It is the nightly custom of every good mother after her children are asleep to rummage in their minds and put things straight for the next morning, repacking into their proper places the many articles that have wandered during the day. If you could keep awake (but of course you can't) you would see your own mother doing this, and you would find it very interesting to watch her. It is quite like tidying up drawers. You would see her on her knees, I expect, lingering humorously over some of your contents, wondering where on earth you had picked this thing up, making discoveries sweet and not so sweet, pressing this to her cheek as if it were as nice as a kitten, and hurriedly stowing that out of sight. When you wake in the morning, the naughtiness and evil passions with which you went to bed have been folded up small and placed at the bottom of*

your mind and on the top, beautifully aired, are spread out
your prettier thoughts, ready for you to put on.

As I read, I realize that Alice is beginning to outgrow the
need for me to rummage in the contents of her mind. It is
becoming progressively more possible for her to fold her
thoughts, air them out, launder them herself. She can choose
what to wear and what not to wear without me. The goal of
good therapy, like good parenting, is autonomy. I read on and
find a description that seems to capture the essence of the
process in which Alice and I have been engaged.

I don't know whether you have ever seen a map of a
person's mind. Doctors sometimes draw maps of other parts
of you, and your own map can become intensely interest-
ing, but catch them trying to draw a map of a child's mind,
which is not only confused, but keeps going round all the
time. There are zigzag lines on it, just like your temper-
ature on a card, and these are probably roads in the island,
for the Neverland is always more or less an island, with
astonishing splashes of colour here and there, and coral reefs
and rakish-looking craft in the offing, and savages and
lonely lairs, and gnomes who are mostly tailors, and caves
through which a river runs, and princes with six elder
brothers, and a hut fast going to decay, and one very small
old lady with a hooked nose. It would be an easy map if that
were all; but there is also first day at school, religion, fa-
thers, the round pond, needle-work, murders, hangings,
verbs that take the dative, chocolate pudding day, getting

into braces, say ninety-nine, three-pence for pulling out your tooth yourself, and so on, and either these are part of the island or they are another map showing through, and it is all rather confusing, especially as nothing will stand still.

Of course the Neverlands vary a good deal . . . but on the whole the Neverlands have a family resemblance, and if they stood still in a row you could say of them that they have each other's nose, and so forth. On these magic shores children at play are for ever beaching their coracles. We too have been there; we can still hear the sound of the surf, though we shall land no more.

Working with Alice in psychotherapy, I get to see the zigzagging map of her mind and explore her island of Neverland alongside her. In so doing I arrive back at my own Neverland as well, revisiting it not from the distance that age causes but from the perspective of a curious adventurer. As I reflect on Alice's upbringing, my sense of sadness ebbs and is replaced by a sense of happiness that I am helping her to grow up.

Later in the story, I discover that Peter Pan was known in Mrs. Darling's day because "when children died he went part of the way with them, so that they should not be frightened." Max's short life and difficult death may have left him stranded on the shores of Neverland forever, but in a way it is a far greater tragedy that his death helped to keep his sister attached to that place, to remain behind with Peter Pan, to never grow up.

In Search of the Cheshire Cat

I think about how my patients, like children, help transport me back to Neverland and how much I enjoy the visit. But I wouldn't want to live there. While it is too early in therapy to know for sure, I wonder if Alice one day will want to leave Neverland forever and join me in the grown-up world that waits for her.

3

The Sea Slug
on the Couch

*I'm driving a large red speedboat to my company
picnic, which is being held on an island, a small
rocky one off the coast of Maine. I drive it right
up to where my boss is standing, and I beach it on
some soft sand. The engine is running smoothly;
it's loud and powerful. When I cut the engine,
everybody is silent; they all stare at me in this impressive craft.*

I'm wondering where the red boat comes from, and how
it is that telling you about it is supposed to help me," says
Ted, after dutifully telling me his dream.

Sidestepping the question, I ask him, "What are your
associations about the red boat?" I grimace a little, because
I realize that Freud has slipped out of my mouth inadver-

tently. Yet despite my ambivalence about the word "associations," which sounds shrinky, associations are precisely what I want.

"I'm not sure. I remember that there was this famous oil well firefighter my father used to tell me about as a kid. He had a big red boat. Whenever we'd pass the boat in the harbor, my father would point it out, saying 'There's Red Adair's speedboat.' My dad was a volunteer firefighter in our town, but this guy Red was a pro. I think my dad sort of looked up to him, thought he was impressive and brave. He'd put out these giant oil well fires all around the world. Dad said he made lots of money because wealthy Arab sheiks would pay him small fortunes to fight oil well fires for them. I guess I pictured him in exotic places, surrounded by women, risking his life, and looking cool and collected. You know, James Bond. His boat reflected my picture of him: it was showy, fire-engine red, larger than life. I think it was called *Trailblazer*.

"And about the company picnic in the dream, I've been telling you how much I'm dreading the real one. Especially the softball game. You know, it's always the bigwigs versus the peewees—those of us who are not so high on the corporate ladder. It reminds me that I'm not as much of a big shot as I'd like to be, as I would have expected to be by now. The softball game also makes me uncomfortable because it's not something I'm particularly good at. After my parents' divorce, I didn't get to practice baseball or football much anymore."

Following a patient's associations in a session is like

browsing in his or her neural netscape, getting the lay of the land by examining the interlocking ideas and images as they spin themselves out. When I ask Ted to say whatever comes to mind, even if it seems silly, embarrassing or irrelevant, I am asking him to reveal as much as he can about how his cortical networks function, to show us which thoughts, feelings, and images are interlinked in the neural web that makes up his mind. He is doing his best to let one idea slide into another, one pattern of activation trigger another. Free association is a bit like a game of pinball, with both Ted and me blind to the layout of the pinball table. Ted plays the part of the pinball, letting his brain bounce around from idea to idea, in the process showing us the topography of the table itself. I function like the flippers, trying to keep the ball in play, using questions to jumpstart the game once again if Ted begins to lose momentum. Like any experienced pinball wizard, I try to use my questions not as random flippers but as specific maneuvers that send the ball back to the areas where I think Ted and I will score the most points, gain the greatest insights about the structure of his mind. In pinball the ball rolls downhill and I am always fighting to keep the ball in play rather than letting it succumb to the laws of gravity. And in the free association I assume that the patient's unconscious is a force to be wrestled with. Ted's defenses operate to prevent him from seeing all the potential sexual and aggressive implications of the big red boat. It is my job to help him keep the ball in play as his defenses try to make it roll down the chute.

Although I have learned in prior pinball games that

there are a finite number of general layouts for the table, there are an infinite number of ways the general layout can be executed. In other words, the overall themes that the story synthesizer can tell are limited, perhaps because humans, born prewired to have relationships with others, tend to have recurrent central concerns. But the elements of the stories are unique to each individual. Even if I have another patient who is concerned about his masculinity, he is unlikely to use the central symbol of a showy red speedboat to tell his tale. The recurrence of central human patterns allows me to gain expertise as I garner experience treating patients in psychotherapy, while the endlessly fascinating variations on individual personal symbols ensure that my work is never dull.

I think of each major symbol in a dream as a nodal point in the network to be investigated; tweak it with a question and find out what it's connected to. Notice how neatly Ted's associations have led us right back to an important relationship, the one with his father during his childhood and how it was affected by his parents' divorce.

The dream images and Ted's associations to them also have highlighted a particular kind of man, the "Red Adair," who is powerful and successful at what he does, self-confident and cocky—qualities the patient has in his dream and would like to possess in real life. Ted also may be hinting that he wishes he had a Red Adair father, a pro, a real man who could teach him how to be a real man as well, so that everyone at work will stop and stare when he arrives. This character is an important one in Ted's repertoire, repeatedly invoked in the tales his story synthesizer authors. Like a Marlboro man straight from central casting, Ted's Red Adair is a powerful protagonist on his private inner TV channel.

I have argued that psychotherapy involves exploring and changing the connections between the interconnected neurons of the upper cortex that make up our minds. Once we take a closer look at the protagonist and other characters, as well as the repetitive twists of plot of our synthesizers, we can then focus on rewriting those aspects shaped by our experience that are no longer useful as we work, play, and love. We understand how a group of simple interconnected processing units could store memories, as well as how one memory state could flow into another. In our Cheshire Cat model, shifting the strengths of the connections between individual neurodes resulted in changes in how ideas were represented and in how they were related to one another within the network. But are the changes we would like to make in the wiring between neurons biologically feasible?

In this chapter I argue that our "wetware," as computer scientists sometimes disparagingly refer to the human brain, has biological mechanisms that make changing the connections between nerve cells possible. I will show you why I think that psychotherapy literally changes the structure of the brain and in so doing alters the way feelings and ideas are interlinked in the mind. Sea slugs may seem a strange place to start in demonstrating the feasibility of what renowned neuroscientist (and psychiatrist by training) Eric Kandel has called the "psychotherapy of the single synapse," but what they have taught us about how neurons change as they learn is amazing.

The sea slugs in question, more technically known as *Aplysia californica*, are a type of marine snail. Their giant nerve cells and their simple circuitry make them ideal for research on neuronal connections. Because they have networks that consist of small numbers of predictably wired neurons, watching their neurons change in response to experience is like watching a computer motherboard in action. You can watch a sea slug's circuitry and see how the connections between cells change as it learns.

Aplysia has a neural pathway similar to the reflex that causes us to jerk our hand away from an unexpectedly hot burner on the stove. Reflexes are relatively primitive, simple neural circuits. They generally consist of a sensory arm (which relays to your spinal cord the information that the burner is hot) and a motor component (which instructs your hand to move quickly). What triggers this response from the snails are starfish, for whom they can quickly become escargots.

Kandel studied the sea slugs' gill-withdrawal reflex. They have a breathing apparatus called a respiratory gill; it is covered by fleshy protective tissue, which ends in a siphon. The slug sucks in water through the siphon, and as the water passes across the slug's respiratory gill, it extracts oxygen. When the siphon is touched, the slug retracts its gill, protecting its crucial respiratory apparatus. This behavioral sequence is generated by two types of circuits. First, there are twenty-four sensory neurons around the siphon that connect directly with the six motor neurons responsible for with-drawing the gill. Second, there are several circuits in which sensory input is sent to "interneurons," which pass the signal on to the motor neurons. Therefore, the entire neural wiring diagram for this gill-withdrawal behavior consists of several two-neuron (sensory-motor) and three-neuron (sensory-inter-motor) circuits.

Imagine three Revolutionary soldiers joining hands to relay information; the first says, "I see one light on the opposite shore, pass it on"; the second runs down from the watchtower and says, "Psst, he sees one light, Paul"; and the third, Paul Revere, gallops off on his horse to sound the alarm. The interneurons relay the sensory information to the motor neurons, causing them to initiate movements in response to the sensation. Although it is very simple, this neuronal circuit in *Aplysia* is capable of two distinct forms of modification that lead to different behaviors—two forms of learning, called habituation and sensitization.

Habituation is a type of learning in which there is a decreased response to a repeated harmless stimulus. In humans, habituation is responsible for capacities such as being able to block out distractions. On a crowded, noisy subway, after a while, the noise and visual stimulation of the crowd recede into the background, and you can become engrossed in what you are reading.

When the sea slug's siphon is touched, its sensory neurons fire. A flurry of electrical current surges down the neuron. At the end of the sensory neuron a neurotransmitter is released, which floods the synapse (gap) between the sensory neuron and the motor neuron. The neurotransmitter latches on to receptors on the motor neuron's surface. If the motor neuron receives enough stimulation from the neurotransmitter, it fires, and the slug's gill retracts. But after the siphon of the slug is touched over and over, habituation occurs, and the slug no longer withdraws the gill in response to the harmless touches to its siphon.

Habituation of synaptic transmission is a bit like the history of transatlantic flight. Lindbergh's success was a first, triggering a parade. But since then, more and more planes have made the trip, and now even the landing of the Concorde isn't accompanied by much fanfare.

How does habituation work on a cellular level? As the sea slug's siphon is touched over and over, the motor neuron that leads to gill withdrawal becomes less and less likely to fire in response to the same touch. As the repeated touching of the slug's siphon continues without an attack by an army of starfish, the slug "concludes" that the touching does not herald anything important. Kandel and his colleagues showed that this habituation occurs because less and less neurotransmitter is produced by the sensory neurons when they are stimulated repeatedly. This decline in neurotransmitter release occurs because the sensory nerve undergoes changes that permit less and less calcium—the substance that controls the amount of neurotransmitter released by a neuron—to enter the cell. With less and less neurotransmitter released, the motor neuron is bombarded by fewer and fewer sorties and thus receives less and less inducement to fire. When the motor neuron doesn't fire, the gill is not retracted in response to the touch. In habituation, it is as if the slug becomes blasé about the harmless touching. You might say it has become downright sluggish. Of course if Paul Revere's ride had happened night after night, he might have ultimately headed to Lexington and Concord at a trot rather than a gallop, too.

With sensitization, the second form of simple learning, the response to a stimulus is heightened by repeated excitation. If a stimulus is noxious, like an electrical shock to a slug's tail, the neural circuit that mediates this behavior is primed to respond more quickly. The neural mechanism by which sensitization occurs is the exact opposite of that which mediates habituation, with one important difference: Becoming habituated to one stimulus does not make a slug ignore all other stimuli; but becoming sensitized to a stimulus does make a slug respond more strongly to all other stimuli as well, even if they are not noxious. In other words, during sensitization, the sensory nerve undergoes changes that permit increased amounts of calcium into the cell, thus causing more neurotransmitter release and a brisker and stronger gill-withdrawal.

No nerve cell connections are created or destroyed by teaching the slug to habituate or to be sensitized to a stimulus. Short-term habituation and sensitization change the functional effectiveness of previously existing connections solely by modulating calcium influx into, hence the amount of neurotransmitter released by, the presynaptic terminals.

But what about long-term learning and memory, the kind we are, presumably, the most interested in when we think about how psychotherapy changes the brain? Having taught their slugs to respond more briskly than they initially did to tail shocks, Kandel and his colleagues next tried to get them to remember to do so indefinitely rather than for just a few hours. They found that when a slug is repeatedly shocked, the same mechanism that leads to changes in the permeability of the cell to calcium also triggers the synthesis of new proteins in the cell. Thus, while short-term learning can occur through simple shifts in the amount of neurotransmitter released, long-term memory actually requires the synthesis of new proteins, using the genetic material in the nucleus of the nerve cell as a template.

Just what do these newly synthesized proteins actually do? Kandel showed that the proteins are building blocks that allow neurons to sprout new neural interconnections in response to experience. In fact, one of the proteins synthesized when a neuron is repeatedly stimulated is nerve growth factor, which sends a powerful message to the neuron to increase its number of branches, thereby increasing the number of connections it makes with other cells. These changes are also called arborizations, because they make the nerve cell look like a bushier and bushier tree. Drugs that interfere with the synthesis of new proteins block this sprouting of new connections and also halt the transformation of short-term into long-term memory. The growth of new connections changes learning from a short-term, functional shift in the effectiveness of a synapse to a long-term, structural change in the branches of the nerve cells, as well as in the number of synapses between the two cells.

You may find the sea slugs fascinating but not quite get what they have to do with Ted, his red boat, and his psychotherapy with me. After all, I cannot slice up Ted's brain to investigate which neurons are connected to which other neurons or to see these connections changing in response to psychotherapy. But I can look for ideas that seem interconnected and then question whether how they are connected makes sense. Though my map of Ted's mind may not yet be at the level of individual neurons, Kandel's slugs strongly suggest that there is a plausible biological mechanism through which changes in neuronal connections, similar to those we saw in neural network models, could occur in the brain.

If I were to try to make a map of Ted's circuitry as revealed in his dream, such a map might read something like this:

1. Ted in dream as powerful, admired at company picnic ⟹ red speedboat reminiscent of powerful masculine firefighter Red Adair ⟹ speedboat somehow dangerous, showy, big

2. Ted in reality as wimp, humiliated during softball game at company picnic ⟹ game as symbolic of Ted's general failure to advance at work ⟹ loss of father as reason for being bad at softball, work

Notice that Ted's associations contain two contrasting self-representations or views of himself—big and powerful, and small in stature, wimpy. These two views seem to be a central organizing feature of his session material, including the dream and his associations to it. The two views of himself are in conflict, with each protecting Ted in some ways and harming him in others. If Ted is big and powerful, others may be envious and perhaps want to take what he has for their own. If he is small and wimpy, he avoids the attacks of others, but he has nothing of value for himself. But in addition to listening to what Ted says in telling me the story of his dream and his associations to it, I listen also for what he does *not* say, seeking to stretch the bounds of my understanding of his neural networks. To do this, I rely on what my own series of associations during the session reveals to me.

I cannot assume my ideas prove anything definitive about Ted, though many therapists do fall into this trap; my associations are my own personal hunches, having perhaps as much to do with *my* experiences and personality as with Ted's. Only *his* associations are legitimate data that help me to define what his networks contain. But because I have studied Ted's mind closely during his psychotherapy, I often find that we are on the same wavelength; my associations are not random, nor are they wholly about myself. During psychotherapy I am taking a map of Ted's networks into my own mind and brain—internalizing it—then using it to chart our course as we work together in psychotherapy. In this case, I find myself thinking:

red boat⟹ 1. I have red hair, does the boat refer to me?

2. The Big Red Boat of Disney World, compromise of adult cruise and family vacation, Mickey Mouse

3. Showboating. Is Ted planning to take a date to the picnic, one who will turn heads, a redhead? Is the power of the red boat somehow connected to his power to win women?

island⟹   1. Off coast of Maine, not a good place to dock a speedboat, not sandy and smooth, rocky— away from Maine (main?) coast, remote

2. No man is an island—how did Ted make it as man without his father around?

softball⟹   1. Not hardball (balls), a "girl" sport

fire⟹   1. Red Adair puts out powerful fires, fires fueled by oil that need containing

2. Ambition is a kind of fire in one's (Ted's?) belly, perhaps driving him but dangerous if released and not contained, perhaps something other men will want to extinguish

3. Fires are raging, perhaps the fire relates to anger

4. Fire is angry red, back to the red boat . . .

Feeling that these fire-related associations on my part are rich and might link up directly both to Ted's conflicted representations of himself as strong or weak and to strong feelings on his part such as anger and ambition, I make my move: "This boat in your dream seems to be a big red symbol of your ambition. But it's as if you're scared of it, as if somehow your ambition to be a big shot at work is dangerous."

"Perhaps," he replies in confirmation, "it's a bit like playing with fire to let everyone see me in a different and more powerful light at the picnic."

Kandel's simple snail reflex pales alongside Ted's neural networks, of course, and comparing a snail circuit and a human cortex is hardly fair. But habituation and sensitization are dissatisfying models for another reason. It is neat to see how these two basic processes work on a cellular level, but they are nonassociative forms of learning. The snail learns about the properties of one stimulus, such as a touch or a shock. Learning gets a lot more fun when it is associative, that is, when it involves learning something about the interrelationship of two stimuli or events. In fact, it is the associative links that Ted has learned through life experience that we are trying to uncover in working with his dream, links among masculinity, athletic prowess, and big boats.

How can we ever expect to figure out what each of the countless neurons involved in such a network is up to? After all, if we put a sea slug on the couch, it will probably just make the couch slimy. A sea slug cannot free-associate so that we can watch its giant neurons in action.

In fact, the simplest model of associative learning is classical conditioning, the type of learning that Pavlov's dogs displayed. In classical conditioning, one stimulus becomes associated with another. You may recall that Pavlov worked with a natural canine reflex to a particular stimulus—salivation to food. Then he paired the dogs' food with a tone, and after both were presented together for a number of trials, the tone alone was enough to make the dogs salivate. A dog's salivation to the tone suggests that its brain now contains a new connection between food and the tone; it associates one with the other and salivates to both.

Kandel modified Pavlov's model to fit his slugs by teaching them to withdraw their siphons in response to shrimp juice, a substance that they normally see as benign. We have seen already that the slugs will withdraw their gills automatically in response to small electrical shocks to the tails. By pairing the shrimp juice to the siphon with a shock to the tail a half-second later, Kandel showed that the slug could learn to associate the two and would ultimately briskly withdraw its gill in response to the harmless shrimp juice alone. Furthermore, this connection was a very specific one. Putting the shrimp juice on the siphon only would lead to gill withdrawal. The snail still viewed shrimp juice placed on other areas of its surface as harmless. The snail has learned not that shrimp juice itself is noxious, but that its arrival on its siphon heralds the shock. In other words, it has associated the two, just as Ted associates masculine power with the big red boat.

Kandel's work strongly suggests that similarly, psychotherapy could produce specific alterations in neuronal and synaptic functioning such as those that occur in response to habituation, sensitization, and classical conditioning in

Aplysia. As Kandel himself postulates, psychotherapy probably initially changes the functional connections among neurons, and then later converts these functional changes into changes in the actual structure of the cerebral cortex itself.

Kandel and his colleagues believe that genetic and developmental processes determine the preexisting connections among neurons in many parts of the brain but leave unspecified the strength with which (and even whether or not) many other connections will be made. When we learn, we change the long-term efficacy of synaptic connections. We alter the effectiveness of already existing pathways by changing the patterns of strength between neurons. And we form new pathways by arborizing our existing neural trees, sprouting new branches, which gives rise to new neuronal connections. As Kandel puts it, "When I speak to someone and he or she listens to me, we not only make eye contact and voice contact but the action of the neuronal machinery in my brain is having a direct and, I hope, long-lasting effect on the neuronal machinery in his or her brain."

Wait a minute, you may be saying. I showed you that repeated experience leads to structural change in the neurons of sea slugs. But that's a far cry from showing you shifts in entire groups of neurons in a human brain. You've probably noticed that I am on the verge of saying that psychotherapy can remake Ted's overall representation of himself as a man. Kandel, the cautious neuroscientist who patiently taught me as a medical student and a psychiatry resident, would probably cringe at that inductive leap. But new data from our closest relatives, monkeys, and even from humans suggest that intensive training can change how even large chunks of the brain operate.

Researchers trained monkeys to use only their second, third, and fourth fingers to rotate a small disk to obtain food. The monkeys succeeded in learning this task and doing it repeatedly over a period of weeks. The researchers then examined the monkeys' brains using a brain-imaging technique called magneto-encephalography, which precisely demarcates the function of the cortex at the level of millimeters. When the researchers examined the space used for the representation of the hand in the monkeys' brains before and after the disk-rotating experience, they found that the intense use of the three fingers and the disuse of the other two brought about dramatic changes in cortical connections. More and more of the representation of the hand was devoted to the three fingers they were using; less and less space was devoted to the other two fingers that were not in use. This is a remarkable degree of neural plasticity, or capacity for change, in the cortical representation of something as concrete as a hand.

In another study, researchers surgically fused the third and fourth digits of monkeys so that the two, once separate, now moved as one. When the digits were separate, distinct areas of the cortex represented each finger. After the fusion, the cortical representation areas of the third and fourth digits had lost all demarcation from one another—merged into one.

In humans with a condition called syndactyly, all the fingers are connected to one another with weblike skin, causing the hands to move as one unit. Also using magnetoencephalography, researchers examined the brains of patients with this condition before and after a surgical procedure to separate the fingers. Before the surgery, the fused fingers were represented as an undifferentiated mass of brain tissue. Afterward, each newly freed finger came to be represented in the cortex as a single digit within a few weeks.

These studies contain both good and bad news for those of us interested in the microsurgery of psychotherapy. The good news is that the adult brain is very plastic, giving us the power to change throughout our lives. The bad news is that the saying "use it or lose it" applies not only to our washboard abs but also to our brains. The systematic workout that psychotherapy provides for the brain requires that we use what we learn—in the world outside our therapist's office, both during and after our treatment.

You also may be wondering to what extent Kandel's work implies that *any* experience changes your mind; how does simply thinking your own thoughts or having a casual conversation with a friend affect your neural networks? Why hasn't Ted been able to sort out his problems on his own or with a friend? Why does he need long-term psychotherapy with me to really change his mind? Perhaps one key to why everyday situations like thinking or talking to a friend usually do not change our minds in the way that psychotherapy can lies in Ted's remark about his first psychotherapy with another therapist: he complained that it felt like "just a conversation." A conversation can change your mind only so much. A memory of a conversation may get stored in your brain the way a run on the treadmill at the gym gets stored in your body, but one ramble through the neurons that make up your mind does about as much for you as one workout.

True brain training requires focused attention to recognizing and challenging the associations your life experiences have led you to construct. It takes repeated pairings of tail shocks and shrimp juice, as it were. By unlinking and deconstructing the problematic patterns of associations encoded in the interconnections of a patient's neurons, I can help him change his mind. But just as random exercises at the gym will not necessarily build or reshape one particular muscle, chance meanderings in your neural networks are unlikely to sculpt a particular part of your brain. Getting a trainer and learning his or her strategies for accomplishing your goal is a good first step toward change, but change nevertheless requires time and the repetition of the useful exercises. In making this analogy, I may seem to be suggesting that a therapist is nothing more than a personal trainer, but a psychotherapist might be seen also as the equivalent of a physical therapist for the brain. The job is far from cosmetic when it involves the repair and rewiring of aberrant brain structures. This rewiring task may sound emotionally bland compared to the experience of working with a therapist; and it may be that the rewiring of your neural networks can take place only in the context of an affectively intense relationship, as I will show later.

The reworking of previously made neural connections takes time and requires shifts in the underlying brain structures that comprise the mind. Understanding which ideas and symbols are interconnected in his mind will help Ted and me to create and destroy links that will change the architecture of his brain. The symbols themselves are the blueprints of the house as it now stands, as well as the guideposts that help us to evaluate how well we are doing on the new structure we are trying to build. We shift neuronal connections around like bricks—laying down new walls, then stepping back to see what progress we have made.

So why doesn't Ted see these connections, rush right out to buy a red speedboat, and enjoy driving it? An old analytic joke asks, "What's the difference between a person with a low IQ and a neurotic?" The answer is that someone with a low IQ can learn from experience. But what interferes with Ted learning to be a hot shot is that he is in conflict, torn between the two types of men our explorations have unearthed. I decide to play up the positive aspects of being a boss to help highlight what it is about being a boss that makes Ted anxious.

"It sounds like in your dream you are a powerful, Red Adair–like man, a man whose power is revealed in this big red showy speedboat," I say to Ted. "You'd like to have that kind of power at the picnic, not to be a wimp but to turn heads, including your boss's."

"Yes," says Ted. "My father was a powerful man, but he didn't teach me his secrets after he and my mother split up. I was never as good as the kids whose fathers were always practicing baseball with them. No matter how desperately I wanted to be good, I couldn't."

"But in the dream you *are* powerful, you have this roaring engine, symbolic of your drive for success, your ambition."

Ted pauses. "You're making me really anxious, talking about that boat so much. I told you the reality of the picnic is that I'll come off like a loser, on the peewee side in the softball game."

About Ted's two portraits of men, which are potential self-representations, you may have noticed that although he complains loudly about the peewee role, he gets anxious about the Red Adair role whenever we discuss it. In fact, he seems to be wedded to a view of himself as a peewee, perhaps as a way of protecting himself from the envy he would engender if he really competed with other men. In fact, if we look in on Ted's progress in therapy one year later, and two years after we began, we quickly see that it has been, literally and figuratively, a profitable time for him; his career, which had plateaued, has begun to take off again. His company's annual picnic approaches again, and this year for the first time he will be playing on the bigwig softball team. He is much closer to being a "big shot" in real life, but being powerful still makes him feel nervous.

Again this year as he tells me about his team assignment, he looks anxious and grim, forecasting that he will probably play badly. But the themes that once lay buried in his dreams, accessible only to my own associations, now are present and conscious in his waking life, on the table for discussion. "Again, it's this same feeling that the softball game will reveal I'm not a real man, not as tough and athletic as the others but soft and less masculine."

"As if you have soft balls?"

"Yes," replies Ted, with a chuckle, "or perhaps no balls at all. My father's leaving has partly to do with that, and so does my mother's tendency to say bad things about him, implying that only a weak man would abandon his family. When she was mad at me, she'd say that we were just alike, me and my dad. I guess I got the message that I was weak, too."

Clearly Ted has learned about what his networks contain, and his capacity to be reflective and insightful about himself is important. But I believe that psychotherapy consists of much more than this, for insight about what is wrong and the capacity for self-analysis rarely are enough to get a person to change. Insight often brings order and comprehensibility to thoughts and feelings that previously seemed chaotic and beyond understanding. But if psychotherapy were to stop here, it would have been successful at changing your mind only minimally. You would be, in effect, learning the algorithms or sets of rules that explain how your networks operate, rather than changing the content and structure of the networks themselves. It would be like watching a rerun of your favorite sitcom on TV, knowing the ending but being unable to change the plot.

Instead, now that Ted and I know who the characters are, we want to push our understanding to the next level, reshape his networks in ways that will make him into the man he wants to be. After learning the rules your networks contain in psychotherapy, the next step is to begin to challenge your character's closely held values, question their operating modes. Now that we have Ted's definition of a "real man" clarified, I decide that perhaps it's time to try to highlight how impossible his definition is. I decide to try a touch of humor.

"No wonder you're anxious," I say. "As I think back to your dream of arriving at your company picnic in your big red boat, it makes me realize once again that in your mind, real men don't eat quiche. You have to be a fearless Red Adair, a man who works and plays dangerously, brashly—with fire—to be a real man. Anything short of hitting a home run with the bases loaded in the bottom of the ninth in the company softball game will make you feel like a little dinghy among mighty speedboats."

Ted chuckles at my overstatement, but he gets the point. "It's *never* enough," he admits sheepishly. "But I guess I did neglect to tell you one other important thing about the picnic. I'm taking Jessica with me. So she'll be meeting the people I've been telling her about these past four months. And they'll meet her."

Jessica is a woman whom Ted recently began dating. I find myself smiling, and thinking that it's always interesting when one of my associations about a patient turns up again, more than a year later, after I have almost forgotten about it. It's amazing that when my patients and I are in sync with each other, our neural networks seem to make contact on a level that I cannot describe in words. At these moments, I can listen to my own associations and they'll lead me in the right direction in terms of how things are laid out in my patient's neural networks. It took a while for Ted to mention bringing Jessica to the picnic, but when he did, I remembered one of my associations to the big red boat in Ted's dream: Ted's new girlfriend, Jessica, has red hair, like me.

4

Teaching an Old Dog
New Tricks

I got a dog!" Chris exclaims excitedly, as soon as the door
to the office closes.

"Congratulations," I say, heading for my chair. I
wonder if this means that Chris, a young homosexual man,
is feeling one step closer to the relationship with a human
companion he wants as well. "I named him Astro, after the
space dog on the Jetsons."

"What's he like?" I ask, with interest. I am curious, after
all our discussions, to learn what kind of dog he has actually
chosen.

"Well, he's a mixed breed, part Newfoundland, part Saint
Bernard. He's really big and furry, friendly and rambunc-
tious," Chris says with a chuckle.

A Newfoundland for a new-found-man. I find myself
playing with the words. A St. Bernard, a rescue dog to save

Chris from his life of loneliness. But such a large dog in a New York apartment? I imagine the dog taking up Chris's whole living room. I picture an oversized pooper-scooper for cleaning up after Astro on Manhattan streets twice a day. No doubt about it, living with a dog in New York City is an intimate proposition. But Chris quickly sets me straight on one aspect of the importance of the dog's size: "He's great to sleep with, almost as large as a person."

I think about my cat, who sleeps like a purring fur hat on my head every night, and I'm glad to know Chris has a new bedfellow of his own.

"And he's really, really friendly, no questions asked."

Not too long ago, Chris felt hesitant about the idea of getting a dog. On the one hand, he was afraid of how attached he might become to it, and on the other, he feared the pet could become a burden, tying him down on the weekends, enslaving him to its needs. This pattern mirrored how he felt about having a boyfriend. When he was alone, he longed to have a partner to share his life. But as soon as he actually started to date someone seriously, he felt smothered and became angry about feeling intruded upon. He was happiest when he was able to retreat to a position of aloof aloneness, convincing himself for a while that he didn't need anyone.

In Chris's current neural-network wiring, relationships always have this theme: to be attached or to care about someone is to be vulnerable to losing them. Far better to stoically endure starving for affection than to put yourself at risk by jumping into a relationship. Far better never to need anyone than to depend on someone and be disappointed if he is not really there when you need him. For Chris, close relationships also still brought with them a sense of having his space invaded. Chris is in his third year of four-times-weekly psychoanalysis, and over time he has gradually come to understand this central theme, this prime-time drama playing daily on his own internal network. We have been working on changing its plot and characters.

In order for his psychoanalysis to truly change his personality, Chris has to let me become a character on the set of his internal drama, let me get inside his head and help him rearrange the furniture. Because Chris knows a limited amount of "real-life" information about me, I am available to play whatever role he wants to cast me in. His casting of me will parallel the way he casts others, including Astro, in the core stories of his cortical story synthesizer. Astro and I are a form of experimental theater on Chris's part, giving him a chance to "workshop" the central script, which he is in the process of rewriting, without committing to a final version yet. He can see whether we are comforting enough to be worth the potential pain our abandonment might bring.

At the moment, Astro and I are starring in not-quite-parallel parts. The contact and closeness Chris seeks from Astro is something he would seek from me if only he could let himself. But I'm harder to have a relationship with than Astro. I won't sleep with Chris, and I talk back. I won't stay or heel when he wants me to.

By getting a dog, Chris is showing us that his internal representations of himself and others are shifting. Before he got Astro, Chris fantasized about bringing the dog to a session, ordering it to stay in my waiting room while he talked with me. I wondered if the idea of leaving his dog in the waiting room might represent a subtle way of being formal with me. Perhaps Chris was keeping me at arm's length, even though I got the feeling he was increasingly attached as well. I pictured the dog lolling on my analytic couch instead, making himself at home. But this image felt unsettling. It brought Chris too close, made me feel as if he was intruding on *me* and *my* space. Was there something about Chris that made me reluctant to let him snuggle up to me? I realized that my image of Astro taking up all of Chris's living room and requiring a jumbo-sized pooper-scooper paralleled my image of the dog lounging on my analytic couch. Too much space, too much shit, too overwhelming to deal with.

As if in response to this, Chris seemed to have a difficult-to-define tentativeness, an awkwardness toward the end of the session that suggested he was acutely aware that he would be leaving soon. Better to be poised to leave, to almost end the session himself a moment early than to feel hurt when I ended it. Better to restrain himself from gobbling up what I had to offer than to allow me to accuse him of feeding too greedily. And yet how could I not warm up to him? Without intimacy, the lifeblood that comes with close human relationships, Chris seemed wan and pale.

I have asserted that psychotherapy changes your mind by altering the connections between neurons in your upper cortex that make up the story synthesizer. I have shown how a network of simple, interconnected neurodes could give rise to complex, interlinking ideas. And I have argued that the model of learning as a process of changing the weights between neurons is not only biologically feasible but actually already substantiated by current research findings. You may have noticed that I have also been saying that your neural networks contain something specific: your model of how relationships work. In this chapter I explain how and why we form prototypes of relationships, and how this process leads, in turn, to the construction of the characters our story synthesizers contain.

Infant-observer Daniel Stern suggests that even early in life we are primed to form prototypes, overall internal maps of events. For example, as the infant feeds at the breast day after day, he learns what it is like to be breast-fed. While each episode of feeding may form a discrete and specific memory initially, over time the multiple feedings tend to blur together to create a basic prototype of breast-feeding—Mom does this and I do that and then this is the result. The infant averages the relatively small variations from feeding to feeding, and thus the map is created.

The utility of these maps—which have variously been known as templates, schemata, representations, and scripts in the psychological literature—seems neurobiologically clear. To the extent that experiences are the same or close to the same, why waste storage space creating new and specific memories of events when averaging them is just about as good? If I go to McDonald's for lunch in four different cities, I needn't memorize the details of each one, such as where the bathroom is and who waited on me or where I sat. Instead I have a schema in mind: I show up, order my burger, pay, wait for it, carry it on a tray to an unoccupied table, and eat my lunch. McDonald's is probably not mother's milk, but like breast-feeding for an infant, McDonald's is predictable and filling, if also ultimately somewhat boring. Knowing what you're getting is part of why the fast-food chain idea works. But Big Macs, like breast-feedings, tend to blend together. Of course, breast-feeding provides a good deal more emotional nourishment than a Big Mac.

Infant researchers have shown that infants do indeed construct such prototypes. In a fascinating study, Mark S. Strauss and his colleagues showed ten-month-old infants a series of schematic face drawings; each face had a different nose length, eye width, or ear length. The infants responded to faces that were more familiar by looking at them for a shorter time than other faces (because they, like our slugs that were touched repeatedly, had already habituated to them). Infants acted most familiar with a picture that was an *average* of all the facial features they had seen even though they had never seen the *actual* averaged picture itself before. In other words, the average of all the faces they had constructed was most familiar to the infants, despite the fact that they had never seen it before.

Of course, if you think back to our Cheshire Cat model, it is not surprising to find out that we construct prototypes. After all, spontaneous generalization and the recognition of patterns are built-in features of networks of interconnected neurons. Daniel Stern argues that early perceptual experience itself is the engine that drives the coalescence of prototypes, including our initial division of the world into self and other. We inevitably begin to notice that the shape that is our mother's head tends to move across our visual field at the same rate as the shape of her torso. If this is more or less invariant, we begin to realize that her head and her torso are connected. We literally begin to sketch her outline as we gain more visual abilities and more and more experience (just like an increasingly well-trained neural network would).

This budding recognition of self and other which is rooted in our daily perceptual experience coalesces earlier in life than you might think. For instance, in one fascinating study, Stern tested a pair of four-month-old female Siamese twins who were connected at the chest and consequently always facing each other. The elegantly simple, ingenious study design turned on the fact that the twins tended to suck on both their own fingers and each other's fingers.

When a twin spontaneously sucked her own fingers, Stern placed one hand on her head and one hand on her hand and gently pulled her fingers out of her mouth. Because the sucking was pleasurable and she wanted to continue, the child resisted his efforts to pull the fingers out of her mouth by flexing the muscle in her arm, thereby creating a counterforce designed to keep her fingers in her mouth.

In contrast, when the twin sucked on her sister's fingers and the sister's fingers were pulled from her mouth, she responded not by increasing the resistance in her own arm muscles but by straining her head forward, seeking to find the other twin's fingers again. In this way, Stern and his colleagues showed that both twins "knew" whether the fingers they were sucking were their own or not.

Stern proposes that they came to know this inevitably because of their natural ability to detect invariance, to notice what does not change. Putting your own fingers in your mouth involves three invariants: (1) you know you want to suck your fingers before you move your hand to your mouth; (2) when you move your hand, your brain tells you your hand has moved through sensory feedback loops that tell you its new position; and (3) your own movements have consistent and predictable consequences in the outside world. In this model, a gradual coalescence of a sense of self and a recognition of self as distinct from other is inevitable.

The first dog prototype that Chris and I discussed in his therapy was Laika, the Russian dog that was sent into outer space all alone in a capsule, a pioneer in the early stages of the Russian space program. Laika's story caught Chris's childhood imagination because it captured aspects of how he felt about himself. He envisioned the dog wasting away alone, cold and scared in the darkness of outer space, orbiting the earth but unable to return to it. This image was not a random one; Chris's father was a NASA engineer, and Chris had grown up in the sixties and seventies, surrounded by the American space program. He wanted desperately to feel close to his father, but instead he felt that he was always orbiting, never landing, never feeling firmly connected. At the beginning of therapy, the space dog's story was a sad one, a tale of hurt and abandonment. If this period had a theme song, it was David Bowie's "Space Oddity," about Major Tom, a man who floats off into outer space alone and untethered.

Over time my perspective on the space dog began to change. Although he was a lonely drifter in outer space, at the mercy of the scientists who launched him, he was also a pioneer. Like Chris, the space dog was self-contained and lonely in a thick insulating capsule that kept him separated from others. But his capsule also protected him—kept him safe, unhurt, and above it all. I suggested that Chris had concluded that it was better to be a stoic adventurer, even if that meant not having close relationships, than to be a lowdown earth dog, begging for scraps of affection. Yet in the space-dog script, Chris is also at the mercy of another, launched into outer space like Laika, in constant danger of being disconnected and left to die alone of starvation in the depths of outer space. Chris is anxious and alone, while the scientists are aloof and unconcerned about him.

These internalized models of relationships with others become the lenses through which subsequent relationships are seen and organized. The internal neural structures on which these representations are based become our de facto reality. Early in psychotherapy, the space-dog relationship representation predominated; Chris imagined me as cold and uncaring, watching him from a detached analytic position, examining him like a bug under a glass while taking notes. In response, he felt anxious and all alone. In fact, he came to therapy seemingly poised to see me as detached and unavailable. He wondered whether I would ever feel any sense of connection to him, whether I would continue to treat him for even one last session if he ran out of money and couldn't pay up. He believed that I never thought of him between sessions and forgot him as soon as he left the room. He worried that I would lose interest and perhaps move away, leaving him behind. He was the guinea pig space dog and I was the mad scientist.

In addition to the fact that our inborn circuitry primes us to create prototypes such as Chris's space dog, there is biological evidence that suggests we are prewired to seek relationships, too. Of course, seeking relationships is a sensible Darwinian thing to do if you are a helpless human infant, because without a caretaker you will not survive. Luckily, babies come with a full arsenal of equipment that promotes interpersonal bonding and the formation of relationships. Using creative study designs capable of eliciting "answers" from newborns, who are nonverbal, Jerome S. Bruner and his colleagues found that infants a few days old preferred human faces to other stimuli; they would perform certain actions to get a projector to show them human faces.

William P. Fifer and his colleagues showed that infants also prefer human voices to other sounds. And it is not just any voice they seek; infants at three days prefer their mother's voice most. When a tape of the mother's voice was acoustically corrected to make it sound as it would have to the fetus in the uterus, researchers were able to show that infants recognized and preferred their own mother's voice on the day they were born!

Similarly, in another study, Bruce A. MacFarlane and his

colleagues showed that three-day-old infants both recognized and preferred the smell of their own mother's milk on a cotton pad to the milk of another woman. The babies showed significantly greater turning of their heads toward the pad with their mother's milk on it and significantly more turning away from the pad with another woman's milk. This preference for humans in general and our mothers in particular is handy if our survival depends on bonding with a caretaker.

We have seen that we have a natural ability to generate prototypes that arises from the built-in properties of our cortical neural networks. And we have explored the evidence that we are primed to seek relationships with humans in general and our mothers in particular at birth. These two defining features of our biologies, taken together, suggest that it is reasonable to conclude we are primed to build prototypes of relationships in early life. Why would we need this ability, and what makes it central?

I have suggested already that we need relationships to survive, because without them we would die of starvation, dehydration, or exposure. But if you think back to Psych 101, you may recall that we need more than nutrients and shelter from our caretakers. In case your Psych 101 went in one ear and out the other like my Calculus 101 did, let me give you a quick refresher. You may have seen those striking movies of baby monkeys who were raised in isolation for the first six months to one year of life. The monkeys look almost like autistic children, crouching in their cages, rocking back and forth, and refusing to play, fight, or have sex with other monkeys. You may recall that giving the isolated baby monkey a cloth-covered wooden mother helped to prevent the severe version of this isolation syndrome, but adding this inanimate mother plus giving the isolated baby a few hours daily with a normal infant monkey who lived in a colony of monkeys was enough to allow normal development to occur.

Similarly well-known studies with humans, conducted by psychoanalyst René Spitz and his colleagues in the 1940s, also suggested that the caretaker–infant relationship is not about just food and shelter. The researchers compared the development of infants raised in a foundling home for abandoned children to that of those raised in a group home by their mothers, who were prisoners. Both settings provided adequate nutrition and hygiene, but each of the women in prison tended to her own baby only, whereas the foundling-home nurses cared for seven babies, none of whom was their own.

At four months of age, the babies in the foundling home did better, suggesting a genetic bias in their favor. But by year two, the babies whose mothers were prisoners walked and talked normally, whereas only two of the twenty-six foundling babies could walk or talk at all. And once the children had missed this critical period in their development, they never recovered. Interaction with involved caretakers is needed for motor and language skills to unfold normally. Perhaps we need relationships to ensure that our prototypes of how to have relationships unfold normally as well.

Over time in Chris's therapy, the dogs that frequently were the subject of our sessions began to change. Not lost in space, the next dog was attached in an angry manner to a heartless master, who emerged as Chris's father. As Chris remembered bitterly the "scraps" of affection that he "begged" from his father during his childhood, he realized that he was still speaking about their relationship in canine terms. He reported being angry at his father for putting him down when he tried to play Little League or when he got less-than-perfect grades. He remarked somewhat anxiously that he would have loved to bite the hand that fed him. But Chris could not snap at his father, even if he was really hurt, because he fantasized that his father would then crush him, either stamp him into submission or refuse to have anything more to do with him. I came to think of the second dog as an Elvis-style hound dog that was literally "a-crying all the time." The hound-dog script showed a different set of self-and-other representations than Laika. Chris was not anxious and alone, but angry; not abandoned, but enslaved. His father was not a cold detached scientist, but a harsh and demanding master.

As the hound-dog script unfolded, aspects of Laika the space dog also came more fully into view. Chris explored his gayness as a kind of treason of sorts; in a community filled with NASA scientists and engineers who formed the core of the American space effort, his space-dog self was Russian. Chris's awareness of being different early in his life, in part because of his "feminine" qualities and in part because of his homosexuality, led him to feel disconnected from his father, and it shaped their subsequent relationship.

As Chris explored the second dog, his relationship with

me gradually began to change. He speculated about the various ways in which I was making him dependent on me, angrily feeling manipulated if I asked to change our meeting times and questioning my motives, which he believed must consist simply of wanting to take his money. He worried that I would become more and more withholding as he became more and more dependent, that he would become enslaved to me just as he felt enslaved to his father while growing up.

"I think that as soon as I would get closer to him, my dad would pull back, just like it seems you're doing now," Chris told me on one occasion. "I remember going to the zoo with him and that he started to pat my head. I liked it, so I reached up and tried to hold his hand. But he said I was too old, that boys my age didn't hold hands with their fathers. I remember feeling embarrassed and ashamed. I guess I think that relationships can only work if I don't want too much, expect too much from them. I've been told by friends that I often seem almost indifferent when I meet a guy I like on the street. It panics me if I feel like I might want or need something from him." Chris pauses for a moment, looking sad. "It reminds me of how earlier in therapy I wanted to quit because I started to realize I was thinking about you and looking forward to seeing you too much. I was wanting more of you, and it felt like you were getting all the power, like I was handing it all over to you. This problem makes me feel like I'm on a leash in all my relationships. Maybe that's part of why I feel tempted to break up with John now. Things are good with him, and I'm starting to feel closer, but now I feel like Astro out for a walk. It's like I'm saying: Please, please, I'll do anything if only you'll pat me. I can see that John isn't trying to make me feel this way, not wanting to put me on a leash, but I feel on a leash anyway. Have you ever noticed how sometimes dogs hold their own leash in their mouths even though their owner has let go? It's like I'm keeping a choke collar on myself, on my own desires and urges." Chris is silent for a moment, reflective.

Daniel Stern argues that the sharing of what he calls "vitality affects" is perhaps the most important interaction that takes place between caretaker and child in early life. Vitality affects convey a way of being, a process rather than a content. An example of a vitality affect is a "rush," the process of crescendoing intensity, whether it be a rush of adrenaline, the feeling evoked by the sound of a powerful wave as it hits the beach, or the physical sensation of riding a horse as it breaks into a gallop. Vitality affects are conveyed by music and other arts as well as interpersonal reactions. The *William Tell* Overture is a musical example of a rush.

There is no clear and consistent mapping of emotions as we usually think of them and vitality affects on to one another. A person explosively bursting into a run and a person explosively bursting into a room are both explosively bursting, but each might be feeling a different blend of joy, anger, or fright. Explosively bursting is a process, a *way* of doing something. Stern posits that the infant, like an audience member at a dance performance, observes and experiences the main vitality affects with which the primary figures in his life go about their daily routines, including interacting with him.

Stern argues that vitality affects are the most important and the main means of communication between parent and pre-verbal child, forming the currency of parent–infant interactions.

In fact, much of early play prior to the development of spoken language is predicated on the sharing of vitality affects between caretaker and infant. When caretaker and infant are sharing vitality affects with each other, they are said to be affectively attuned. This communicative attunement often occurs when the caretaker imitates the child's predominant vitality affect in another sensory mode.

Stern gives an example in which a child reacts to a jumping jack popping out of its box by flapping his hands furiously. An attuned and communicative mother will take up his frenetic surprise and translate it into another sensory modality, perhaps by raising and lowering her eyebrows while saying "Ee-oo-ee-oo!" in rhythm with his flapping. Her vocalization captures and mirrors the pattern or process of the infant's hand movements, translating his excitement from the motor to the sensory realm. In other words, the parent demonstrates his awareness of the child's current way of being through a kind of translation from one sensory domain to another.

You may be wondering if an infant could "get" the parent's mirroring of his hand movements in the auditory realm so early in life. There is evidence that suggests that infants have a hardwired ability, called cross-modal perception, that enables them to make such a translation. In one study by Kristine S. MacKain and others, infants were shown two films, one of which corresponded with a soundtrack being played simultaneously. The infants preferred to watch the film that was in sync with the soundtrack, suggesting that they can indeed recognize similar patterns expressed in different sensory modalities.

Examples of vitality affects are ubiquitous in early care-taker–child interactions. In one study, Stern and his colleagues videotaped mothers playing with their children as they would at home. The researchers found that vitality-affect expressions occurred in the infants at a rate of about one per minute. About half the time, mothers showed an attunement response to these expressions; in other words, the mother was reflecting to the child an understanding of his current way of being about once every two minutes. When the mothers were shown a videotape of themselves and their babies at play and asked why they responded as they did to the infant, they typically said they were trying to "share the infant's experience." Stern postulates that these early care-taker–child interactions help babies begin to recognize that internal feeling states are important parts of human experience. As he puts it, "What is at stake here is nothing less than the shape of and extent of the shareable inner universe."

I think that the sharing of vitality affects is often one of the most important connections between me and my patients. The tone of voice with which I ask a question or make a comment, my rhythms and melodies and the way I try to mirror what I am hearing from the patient, can be so important that they even overshadow what I am saying—because during psychotherapy with me, the patient is learning a new way of having a relationship. And that means learning novel ways of relating and connecting. Perhaps it is not surprising that these are the moments of connection that patients tend to recall most fondly when psychotherapy ends.

While Stern recognizes the profound importance of relationships, he does not speculate that shared positive affective states are actually part of our primary motivation for forming relationships in the first place. I think a desire for the warmth that comes with human contact is often a reason that patients seek therapy, and that the therapeutic relationship, like the one with early caretakers, is often a powerful reinforcer because it produces intense and powerful feelings. Affects may actually be a driving force in our lives that motivates behavior, including seeking relationships.

Part of Chris's problem is that he cannot imagine a way of being in a relationship without a power differential. In his neural-network model of relationships, one person is always master, while the other is enslaved. What Chris and I are working on changing, then, is his sense of how two people can be together. Although you still can see the outlines of the master–slave paradigm, Astro the cartoon dog is warmly and affectionately attached to his master, George. The two run together on the treadmill every day, and Astro licks George's face without fail when he returns from work.

When Chris came into therapy, he was quietly despairing but resigned about the idea that he could never quite connect to anyone he cared about. Of course, his decision to enter therapy and to relate to me suggests he had not completely given up, but he seemed firmly rooted in the defensive posture that relationships were not worth the risk of being vulnerable and losing something he cared about. They were also not worth the price of humiliation and domination. In getting Astro, Chris is showing that he has changed; a relationship could now be worth it, even though it could someday end. Chris has sidestepped the master–slave problems in choosing a dog. The roles remain clear-cut, and Chris is the master. But he is toying with allowing himself to be more warmly and collaboratively attached to Astro.

Astro is a far cry from Laika, but he is descended from the Russian space dog and the Elvis hound dog as well. Chris has gradually rearranged the image of himself being launched into outer space by a father to whom he cannot feel connected into a more positive version of the story. Astro is still a space-age dog, but a more connected and exuberant one, one with a real family, the Jetsons. He has a happy-go-lucky mentality, an easy connectedness Chris probably still envies, or perhaps strives for. What is really different between Laika and Astro is the vitality affect with which they connect to those around them.

Astro is not a Russian, a foreigner in outer space. He is almost an Astronaut, an adventurer in the spirit of his father. It is not only the representation of the dog, of Chris himself, that has changed. Chris's picture of his father and of me has shifted gradually as well. Perhaps most important, the feeling he now experiences as flowing between himself and his remembered father and between himself and me has begun to change from an awkward, indifferent aloofness to a warm sense of attachment and affection. Along with the succession of dogs that represent Chris himself, the canine trio, I can see evidence in the material of the psychotherapy that Chris's representation of his father is changing as well. Gradually it has become apparent that Chris's father is more than an obsessional engineer; at times he comes across as a genuinely warm man to whom Chris does feel quite attached. In fact, it may be that Chris's view of his father as distant or dominating helped Chris to disguise his own intense feelings of attachment and attraction. Chris may have been making his father distant and unavailable partially to disguise his own deep-seated feelings.

Chris began to recall with fondness that his father took him to see baseball games in Houston (home of the Astros, I recall with delight). Chris might not have been good at playing baseball, but he was certainly good at learning who the players were. Only in retrospect, from the position of an adult who acknowledged his homosexuality, did Chris appreciate the full meaning of his boyhood crushes on baseball players. Baseball was both something he and his father could share and a socially sanctioned arena in which Chris was allowed to display a keen interest in the players.

As Chris's view of his father shifted, his view of me changed as well. After two years of feeling that I was purposefully withholding and aloof, trying to prevent him from attaching too strongly to me, or that I was enslaving him by fostering his dependence on me, Chris began to feel more clearly that I was on his side. While our relationship provided a laboratory in which his inner portraits of himself and his

father were reawakened, I continued to show up for work
with him and do my best to reflect back to him my sense of
what was happening between us. This repetition of old relationship patterns is essential to change in psychotherapy. In
fact, at the core of neurosis is the fact that a patient repeatedly experiences new relationships as if they were just like old
ones. Thus practice leads not to change but to repetition. The
difference in psychotherapy is that I am repeatedly pointing
out to Chris what he is doing as he desperately tries to make
his new relationship with me fit the old mold. As he under-
stands his own motives, the forces inside him that are shap-
ing his relationships become less tenacious, and he is able to
make different choices. As therapy progresses, practice leads
not to repetition, but to change. An equally important aspect
of the relationship between me and Chris revolves around the
fact that I am there when I say I will be there, listening my
best, trying to understand even the most fierce power struggles he wants to engage me in rather than blindly participat-
ing in them.

The fact that we form prototypes of how to have relationships has several practical implications. First, prototypes
make the psychoanalytic emphasis on early life experiences
with caretakers make sense: each one of the first ten interactions I have with someone will play a larger part in my formation of relationship representations than each of the next
ten. And I am more affected by my McDonald's experience
the first time than the millionth; if you don't agree, just con-
sider the Hungarians' excitement in 1989, as they happily

consumed their first hundred burgers in their new, neon-lit McDonald's in the heart of old Budapest.

Second, prototypes handily help to eliminate the notion that a parent should be perfect. If representations are formed through the averaging of experiences across thousands and thousands of interactions with significant others early in life, a parent need only be "good enough"—a phrase coined by British pediatrician-turned-psychoanalyst D. W. Winnicott. If a parent is good enough, normal object relations can unfold. Notice that Winnicott's phrase itself connotes just the kind of averaging that Stern proposes when he explains how object-relations representations are made.

Third, prototypes suggest why change takes time. It is not that you can't teach an old dog new tricks, but simply that the more experience you have doing something one way, the more repetitions it will take to change that prototype. The older the dog, the more trials it takes to chip away at the representation and little by little to shift a prototype that has already been formed.

When you think about the implications of prototype formation, you may begin to wonder how we ever change at all. Even if we go to psychoanalysis for 45 minutes four times weekly, we are spending only 3 of our approximately 112 waking hours per week trying to change our minds. That's less than 3 percent of our time! And our representations need many repetitive interactions for our well-established averages to begin to shift, many trials before they really begin to change. Luckily, practicing new ways of doing something is not limited to our psychotherapy sessions alone. As we gain insight about what happens in our relationships, we learn to notice similar patterns in life outside psychotherapy and to work on these as well.

Gradually Chris began to talk about the emotional advantages of being a dog, remarking, "Dogs can't hide their emotions. Everything they feel seems to be right there on the surface. They wag their tails when they are happy, they hound you for special treats, and they bring their leashes to you when they want to go out for a walk. When they like you, they act like they do. I'd never do any of that in a relationship." I smiled, because I'd already begun to feel that Chris's grin when I went out to get him in the waiting room showed that he was happy to see me. And in almost every session he showed me how he was carrying my comments from prior sessions around with him, worrying them as if they were meaty bones. He was beginning to think about me and our relationship more outside of sessions, and I could almost watch his internalization, his taking in of me, in action. It started with his triumphant exclamation: "I knew you would say that," and progressed to "I thought you would think x about it," as he told me of an episode that had occurred outside of a session. Finally, the aspects of me that Chris had taken in really became his own, and he would say, "I thought x about it." Aspects of me and how I think about relationships became visibly present in Chris's mind and brain.

"You know, my father took me to look at puppies, because I was supposed to get one for my twelfth birthday, and I wanted a chow chow," Chris told me one day. "They look like little lions, soft but also tough; I'd seen one once, and then I read all about them. They were the working dogs of the Chinese nobility. I found the puppy I wanted about a month before my birthday, and I used to go and visit him at the pet store. I got my history teacher to help me find a name from the Manchu dynasty, the name of a prince.

"But then just before my birthday my parents told me they were getting divorced, and my dad moved out. Mom was so depressed, and she was really mad that my father had taken me to the pet store and let me pick out a puppy. She wouldn't let me get him because she said it was just another thing for her to do, to feed and brush and walk a dog. I swore I would do it myself, but she didn't believe me, and I couldn't get one at Dad's house either, because I only saw him every other weekend.

"I guess I must have felt that my father had just vanished after he moved out," Chris continued. *As if into outer space*, I muse, *into orbit. Hey, wait a minute, didn't the Jetsons have another dog—named Orbit?* I find myself silently singing the Jetson theme song to try to figure it out. "Meet George Jetson; his boy, Elroy; daughter, Judy; Jane, his wife . . ." Distracted by my own association for a moment, and unsure about why I'm singing to myself in a session, I almost miss what Chris says next.

"So," he says consulting his watch and determining that our session is nearly at an end, "John is picking me up in your lobby after the session. He's bringing Astro with him. Do you want to meet them?" Chris is offering to introduce me to his family, just like in the song.

"What do you think you'd feel about introducing them to me? And me to them?" I say, moving the Jetsons to the back burner, returning to my analytic attitude. "Well, I'm not sure," Chris replies. "I guess I have to be sure I'm keeping them both before I let you in on it." Chris laughs, eager to pass this last remark off as a joke. I feel a bit taken aback to hear Chris talk about John and Astro as if they were merchandise that can be returned. But he still feels somewhat tied down by his family, resentful of their demands. "Anyway, you could always meet them later," Chris volunteers. We both smile, and I let him know that we have to stop here for today.

5

An Affective Apprenticeship

I'm in a room with my mother. She's lying very still on a bed. I can't tell if she's breathing or not. The floor of the room is made of stone. The walls are stone too, bare and bleak. Somehow I know it is my job to sweep up the floor. There is a patch of light from a window on the floor, but the room is otherwise dark. I feel hesitant and afraid to sweep around the patch of light. I almost expect that as I sweep it up it will be like in a cartoon: the light will become smaller and smaller until I have swept it into a pinpoint and it disappears. I get into bed, put my head under the covers with my mother. She is very still, but warm—comforting. Suddenly there is a blackbird walking on top of the covers, poking its beak into them. I am scared it will come

under the covers and peck at me or my mother. I
want to run out of the room to get away from it,
but I can't leave my mother by herself.

I t makes me uncomfortable, telling you that dream," says Rob, a married painter in his mid-forties who began analysis four years ago to work on his chronic depressive symptoms and to enable himself to overcome his work inhibition and fulfill his potential as an artist. "I mean, not uncomfortable exactly, but I guess it's making me very anxious. My mouth feels dry . . ." he trails off, and he swallows hard. "I guess the most striking part about it is this thing with the light, the idea that I'll snuff it out and it will be completely dark in the room. I'm leery of sweeping it up, but it's my job. The blackbird is scary; I'm not safe even under the covers. I'm scared and I want to get away from it, but I'm torn, because how can I leave it to peck away at my mother?"

Rob pauses, regrouping and taking a deep breath, perhaps to fight off his anxiety. "The scene itself is depressingly bleak. It reminds me of that scene in *Fantasia*, you know, the Sorcerer's Apprentice, where Mickey Mouse orders the broom to do his work, and once he starts it with a magic spell, he can't stop it."

I recall the scene, the broom carrying bucket after bucket of water at Mickey's behest, and I find myself picturing an industrious young Rob in a Mouseketeers hat, responsible for carrying endless buckets of his mother's tears. An impossible task with such a depressed mother as Rob's—no matter how many buckets he carries, there are always more and more tears to be carried away. They threaten to flood the room. And the crow—is it a symbol for the depression that's a threat to Rob as well as to his mother? Rob has a strong family history of depression on his mother's side, and has himself been taking the antidepressant Prozac for several years. I wonder if the dream shows one view of the depressed mother of Rob's childhood who took to bed for weeks at a time, probably with similar symptoms, often ordering Rob to do chores around the house and to take care of her.

In the last chapter I described the importance of caretaker-infant experiences in teaching the child how to be in a relationship and how to share vitality affects. I also asserted that the sharing of these processes or ways of being is important in the psychotherapeutic relationship as well. In this chapter I present evidence that something even more fundamental and radical is going on between caretaker and child as well as between therapist and patient. As Myron Hofer—a researcher who studies the psychobiology of attachment—puts it, the caretaker serves literally as an external regulator of the structure and neurochemistry of the child's maturing brain. And as researcher Allan Schore proposes, the capacity to experience a full range of affective states and the ability to self-regulate the intensity of affects arises directly from the child's early life experiences with primary caretakers. Even more radical, these early life experiences directly affect the maturation of evolving neuronal circuits between the cortex responsible for representations and the limbic area of the brain responsible for emotions.

There is new and exciting evidence to suggest that the capacity to experience a broad range of affects, as well as the ability to self-regulate affect, has its origins in the interactions of caretaker and infant and arises directly from the maturation of neurons in the cortico-limbic areas of the brain in the first three years of life. While mothers were the primary caregivers in most of the studies I discuss in this chapter, there is no reason that another primary caregiver or even a small group of caregivers could not provide the same function for the growing child. But the maturation of the brain circuits in question is indeed strongly dependent on the quality of the child's early relationships.

Schore suggests that the caregiver conveys her affective response to the infant during the first year of life partly through eye contact. He argues that infants have a fixed-focus visual system at birth that enables them to see most clearly objects that are about ten inches away. Most care-takers instinctively hold their babies—you guessed it—about ten inches away from their faces. As I mentioned in the previous chapter, babies are prewired to prefer faces to other stimuli and to respond to the mother's face in particular. In return, mothers tend to gaze for long periods at their babies; and the infant's gaze reliably evokes a reciprocal gaze from the mother. It is likely that these shared moments of gazing are a crucial and intense form of early interpersonal communication and bonding that predate vitality affects.

Schore argues that when a mother looks at her infant's eyes, her own pupils dilate, a signal conveying pleasure and interest. And viewing enlarged pupils in the mother elicits pupillary dilation in the baby. Together, then, when the infant and mother gaze at each other, the reciprocal gaze triggers an upward spiral of contentment and pleasure, a state that psychoanalysts call blissful symbiosis between mother and child. These "mirroring gaze transactions" of early life seem to serve the purpose of amplifying positive affect. Self psychologist Heinz Kohut proposed that the child's self develops when he sees his reflection in the "gleam in the mother's eye." Perhaps this gleam is more than just a metaphor.

The intense experience of the mother-infant gaze has a built-in cutoff mechanism, gaze aversion, through which either the mother or infant can terminate the surge of positive feeling that gazing evokes. By looking away, the mother can regulate the intensity with which she stimulates her baby. During the baby's early life, an attuned mother matches, then amplifies, and finally stabilizes the infant's positive emotional state. By gazing at the child, she keeps him within an optimal range of pleasurable and excited arousal. And through gaze aversion, she prevents the upward spiraling of positive emotion from continuing to escalate until the infant is overstimulated, spinning out of control. Over time she allows the intensity levels that the baby experiences to become gradually greater, encouraging expansion of the level of emotion the infant can comfortably tolerate. Perhaps eyes are indeed the mirror of the soul. The gazing of mother and infant is not unlike the gazing of lovers.

As this process continues over the first year of life, the baby gradually accomplishes two major tasks. First, he learns to tolerate increasingly intense states of positive emotion, such as elation, without finding them disorganizing. Second, he begins to learn to regulate the intensity of positive affects on his own.

During the first year of life, the portion of the cortex located in the right frontal lobe, known as the orbitofrontal cortex, is developing. It is receiving projections from a lower brain area in the limbic system, which is responsible for emotions, and it is sending neurons back to the limbic system, creating a loop through which the cortex can increasingly serve as a regulator of emotion.

Schore suggests that the nature of mother-child interactions during the first year of life not only has an immediate effect on the infant's affective state, but also leaves a long-term imprint on the structure of this evolving cortico-limbic circuit. Interestingly enough, the developing cortico-limbic circuit uses the neurotransmitter dopamine at its ascending synapses. These dopaminergic circuits are known to be important in pleasure- and reward-seeking behaviors throughout life. High levels of dopaminergic stimulation of the orbitofrontal cortex lead to an emotional state of interest, excitement, and joy. Dopamine also powers the toddler's desire for self-exposure, that "look at me" quality found in toddlers that is accompanied by fearless exploration and a sense of omnipotence and grandiosity. As Margaret Mahler, an infant observer interested in attachment, said of the toddler at this time in his life, the world is his oyster.

The theory of the development of this experience-dependent brain circuit during the first year or so of life dovetails nicely with the results of one study that showed that 90 percent of all caretaker-child interactions in the first year of life were affectionate, caregiving, or playful situations characterized by the caretaker's amplification and sharing of positive affects. Once formed, the cortico-limbic circuit allows the child to experience and to begin to learn to regulate positive affects like elation for himself.

The development of this pleasure circuit occurs in an upward spiral of growth promoting further growth. For example, dopamine puts the neurons into high gear, chemically inducing their growth. This potential for growth means that the neurons are primed to forge the connections that will encode the toddler's evolving internal representations of himself and important others. In turn these representations allow the child to invoke pleasurable states for himself and to regulate their intensity.

I find myself worrying. It's mid-November, the time of year when Rob's depression usually sets in. I think about how he came for treatment four years ago, about this time of the year, feeling flooded by sadness and anxiety. I also wonder whether the scene in the dream contains the seeds of the anger that I think Rob may have felt toward his mother. Being a rescuer is an impossible task, one that ultimately must have made him resent the rescuee, especially since she was too depressed even to begin to help him. Hints of the anger show through in the dream. Might not he have wished at times that she were dead and that he were freed from responsibility for her? Is his anxiety about snuffing out the light a hint not only of his fear that she will die but also of the matricidal feelings he may have harbored?

And what about the dream in relation to me? I wonder if Rob is feeling fearful that I will get sick, go away, or be overcome by sadness and depression myself. He might then be again in a position of rescuing a woman who is supposed to be taking care of him even though he himself is in need of rescuing. I think about how he said two sessions ago that I looked tired, and I remember that a couple of weeks ago I canceled two sessions because I was sick. I wonder whether he needs to have his Prozac increased. I find myself toying with the idea of seeing him five times weekly instead of four. After all, I rationalize, Freud saw his patients six days a week. Meanwhile, on the couch, Rob has lapsed into a listless silence.

One way to see Rob's dream is as a snapshot of his relationship with the depressed mother of his childhood, who desperately needed a rescue of which he was not capable. Other images clearly belong in this section of the "photo album" that Rob and I are working on, the scrapbook that tells the story of his life in terms of relationships. For example, early in treatment Rob showed me his favorite painting, which he said was about his relationship with his mother. In the painting a small girl in a black dress stands before a male harlequin dressed in brightly colored silks, who smiles broadly and extends his hand toward her. Rob is the big one, the one in charge of entertaining, cheering his mother up. He is colorful and larger than life, while his mother is the small, frail other dressed in black. His self is vibrant, energetic. His mother is weak, almost lifeless. The image tells the story of attempted rescue from depression; the two figures are linked together by the mother's sadness and the son's attempt to infuse her with life and exuberance. In the painting, it's hard to tell whose affect ultimately prevails and whether Rob's rescue attempt works.

Whoa, wait a minute, I tell myself. As a psychotherapist (and because of my experiences as a patient in psychotherapy and later in psychoanalysis), I have learned a thing or two about myself, and I have noticed an important invariant: whenever I find myself thinking of Prozac and Freud together in the same sentence, considering simultaneously increasing a patient's medicine and the number of times I see him per week, it is a bad sign. Usually when I go down this yellow brick road, this thought pathway, it shows me that I want to pull out all the stops, to rescue the patient myself.

One of the interesting things about object-relations theory is the notion that representations of self and other complement each other, fit together to make a story. Rob is the white knight to his mother's damsel in distress. She needs rescuing, and he is willing to risk his life to try. Meanwhile, the alligators in the castle moat are nipping at his heels; rescue is a dangerous business.

These self-object representations seem to have been taken in as one to our minds and brains, there to be internalized as an intact, complementary unit. In other words, Rob is familiar with both roles in the story of his dream, and both have found their way into his neural networks because they were taken in as a unit: the self-representation and the representation of the m(other), as well as the emotions that accompany them. In fact, if you have paid careful attention to the effect of his dream on me, you may have noticed that there has been a subtle reenactment of these rescuer-rescuee roles in my relationship with Rob. In the *content* of the session, Rob is telling me about being a frustrated caretaker for a depressed mother who cannot muster the wherewithal to help herself. But in the *process* of the session, Rob has become like his depressed, helpless mother, in need of rescue by me. He has me thinking about pulling out all the stops and saving him.

This role reversal may have several psychological purposes, one of the most important being, perhaps, that Rob manages nonverbally to convey to me a sense of how it feels to be him, overwhelmed, worried, and inadequate to help his mother to the degree that she needed help. I am feeling a version of what he may have felt about his mother and perhaps about himself; no amount of Freud or Prozac is enough. It is possible also to see how internalizing a particular role and its complement as a unit explains some thorny psychological problems such as how the victimized can at times act like the victimizers they vow they will never become. You would think that once abused, a victim would know how horrible the abuse feels and would go out of his or her way not to be abusive. However, many abuse victims end up becoming abusers of others. For every masochist there is a sadist—not only in the external world as it was experienced in the past, but in the masochist's own brain, mind, and self as well!

Recognizing that this role reversal has occurred and that

An Affective Apprenticeship

Rob is conjuring up the scene described in his dreams is helpful; having insight about what I am feeling and what role I am cast in helps me to get beyond my own feelings of desperation. It helps to transport me back into a state where I can analyze—understand what has happened between Rob and myself, see how it parallels his early life situation, and then reflect it back to him for his further elaboration. But first I take a moment to let my mind wander, to allow myself to regain my center before I proceed. I have an amusing image of myself weighed down with a lifetime supply of Prozac in one hand and all twenty-four volumes of the standard edition of Freud in the other, rushing to Rob's rescue. I find myself thinking about the billboard I saw while driving from the hospital to my private office. On the sign Tom Brokaw assumes an up-close-and-personal pose. He seems warm, inviting, as if watching him will be like getting your news from your best friend, only your best friend happens to be a sexy anchorman for NBC. I feel relieved, with only a slight pang of guilt for thinking about Tom Brokaw's sex appeal during Rob's session. I am not yet sure what Brokaw has to do with Rob, but the ironclad grip of the rescuer-rescuee model, whose power lay in the intense negative affect of desperation it generated in me, is definitely broken.

Having stepped outside the role in which I have been rather surreptitiously cast, I can now give Rob notes, like a codirector critiquing a play from the mezzanine. This flipping from actor to director on my part, as well as on Rob's part, is critical. Analysts refer to these two positions as the observing and experiencing egos, and they are the two oscillating ways of being in a psychotherapy session that help it to move forward. In the experiencing situation, Rob evokes in me a sense of how overwhelmed and desperate he felt. I feel overwhelmed and desperate, pressed to act as if I am in the midst of an emergency, while Rob feels numbed out and dead, as if he isn't even here. This phase is essential in getting me to understand what is happening emotionally within the session. When I step back into the observing position, I can see this ghostly dynamic from Rob's past literally reawakened in the session. Because I am no longer in the middle of feeling desperate, I can point out the pattern to him.

As an infant enters the second year of life and becomes a toddler, his evolving mobility leads to a variation on the positive amplification theme. Like a teenager who has yet to learn how to manage his allowance, the toddler, after venturing off into the world without the mother, comes back emotionally spent. He is then refueled by the mother's amplification of positive affect—transformed from a depleted to a reactived state, ready for further forays into the world. These mother-child interactions lead to both the strengthening of the cortico-limbic circuit itself and the continuing construction of internal representations of self and other that coexist with and are linked to positive affective states.

As we all know, when a child approaches two, the party is over, at least for the moment, as far as positive affects go. All hell breaks loose. In fact, one study showed that the number of mother-toddler interactions that involve prohibition increases sharply and that toddlers receive a prohibition from their primary caretaker about every nine minutes. That's a lot of correction; no wonder everybody's cranky during this period. The caretaker begins to focus more on socialization of the child, on developing and expanding his capacity for impulse control, holding him increasingly accountable for his actions.

Schore hypothesizes that the mother's facial expression of distaste and disdain for those behaviors of the child that she is attempting to eradicate creates an experience of affective misattunement rather than the positive elation the child has come to expect. While Schore focuses primarily on facial expression as he did earlier on gaze, lack of response or angry words probably also can trigger the "sudden shock-induced deflation" of the toddler's positive affective state. In essence, the caretaker slams on the brakes, sending the child into a shame-filled, negative, low-arousal state that he is not yet capable of regulating for himself. The child who has been thrown into this state looks like a wet dishrag, limp and ashamed, with little or no body movement. He looks dejected, as if his bubble has burst. Put in terms of Stern's vitality affects, the child has gone from cruising at sixty to stopped in his tracks in one quick moment.

The ability of the caregiver to reengage the child and to repair the rupture in the relationship that her disapproval caused is just as crucial as the disapproval itself. Without disapproval, the child cannot be educated about what he should and should not do, and he remains fragile and overly dependent on the praise of others. But without repair, the toddler is left for a protracted time in a state of deflated negative emotion. Through this process of disapproval and reconnection, the early caretakers teach the child to tolerate and self-modulate increasingly intense negative affects.

As you might have guessed, a second cortico-limbic circuit is developing during this period, in a part of the brain adjacent to the first loop. When the caretaker unexpectedly disapproves of something the child does, the stress of her mis-attunement triggers the release of the stress-related hormone cortisol. Cortisol probably then promotes further maturation of the orbitofrontal cortical loop. In addition, the descending cortico-limbic neurons in this second loop use the neurotransmitter epinephrine, which promotes their acting as a brake on the infant's elation.

Schore postulates that the growth of this new circuit is influenced by the disapproval-repair cycle between child and caretaker characteristic of this period. He cites evidence that suggests that the neurons in this second circuit actually grow faster and better when the child is in a low-arousal state such as the one aparently produced by the caretaker's disapproval. The caretaker of this period is not only exercising the infant's capacity to be more separate and self-regulating but also is literally sculpting this second set of neuronal connections that the child will use for the self-regulation of negative affects over time.

You may have noticed that I have been talking up to now as if all infants are created equal; we now know that this is far from true. Jerome Kagan and his colleagues observed 400 four-month-old infants and categorized them as inhibited or uninhibited. The infants were exposed to various unfamiliar things and people, and observers rated their level of fearfulness. Kagan showed that about one-third of the infants were highly reactive, exhibiting more significant increases in heart rates as well as other expressions of fear. Follow-up of a subset of these inhibited children showed that they remained more fearful and reactive at age four. A study of sets of twins showed also that identical twins were highly likely to be either both inhibited or both uninhibited, suggesting a genetic contribution. As you might imagine, having a highly reactive child who is more easily upset and more difficult to comfort might also have an impact on the caretaker-child connection, and therefore the developing cortico-limbic loops. In addition, a highly reactive child may take longer to form the cortico-limbic loops needed to regulate his excessive amount of reactivity for himself.

Both the cortico-limbic circuits that develop in the first two years of life are found in the *right* hemisphere of the brain, which generally is thought to be important in the regulation of emotion. After age two, a third cortico-limbic circuit is forged, this time from the prefrontal cortex of the *left* hemisphere of the brain down to a group of cells known as the locus coereleus, which in turn project back to the cortex. Schore proposes that this third loop, maturing alongside evolving language abilities, participates in the development of verbally mediated affective and mood states. It gives rise to a more conscious processing of emotional material, which is typical of the left brain, and which allows for the emergence of more verbally mediated emotional states such as anxiety and guilt, which are more advanced emotions than elation and shame.

Schore points out that during this period of development, the child typically seeks the father or another adjunctive caretaker and forms a strong attachment to him. He speculates that perhaps the attachment to someone other than the mother helps to produce the chemical substrate and experience necessary to complete the development of this third circuit for affective modulation.

As these three cortical circuits mature in sequence, the child is all the while forming more and more complex representations of his caretakers and his interactions with them. He can evoke them during separations for purposes of feeling elated, soothing himself, or keeping himself out of trouble. Children ages two to three often are seen doing things that suggest they are evoking internal representations. For instance, a toddler may sing both parts of a song she frequently shares with mother to generate positive feelings or to ward off anxiety in the face of separation. A child may reach out with one hand to swipe a forbidden cookie, then stop herself with the other hand. Over time, internal imagery in the form of stored, emotionally laden representations of the child and the caretaker increasingly help the child to regulate impulsive behavior.

I have been so engrossed in my own Brokaw fantasy that I find I have missed out on what Rob was saying. "I'm sorry, I think I missed what you just said."

"Oh, it's funny you should say that because I was saying

that I feel like you've been less interested in me lately, and it's making me upset and angry at you."

"So my asking what I missed shows that your suspicions are correct?"

"Yes, in a way. It's hard to explain in words, because it feels fundamental, like we're just not on the same wavelength anymore. I feel like maybe you're distracted or maybe you've given up on me, decided I'm a hopeless case. I feel like you're about to bail out on me and I'll be stuck taking care of myself." Rob shifts uneasily on the couch. "In fact, in a way I guess I have already acted like I have to take care of myself. I did something I need to tell you about. I increased my Prozac. I know I should have asked you, but the bottom line is that I didn't. It means I'll run out of my prescription sooner than I should, and you'll have to give me another one. I realized that even if you told me not to increase the medicine I would probably do it anyway." Rob laughs nervously. There is a long, palpably tense moment of silence before he continues.

"You're probably mad at me now. Maybe you'll refuse to give me a new prescription as a way of saying that you're not going to let me be the one in charge of my medication."

"I may see you as a threat to my power?"

"Yes, and you'll want to put me in my place." Like the sorcerer with his apprentice, I think.

"Or else you'll feel resentful and burdened by me, like I'm an ungrateful parasite," Rob says softly, on the verge of tears.

"I might feel about you the way you might have felt sometimes about your mother?" I say gently, aware that my words will probably sting. Rob's only answer is tears, guilty tears that roll down his cheeks. Rob's mother is not the only one who has endless buckets of tears to shed.

When Rob returns the next morning for his session, his concern that I will be angry with him and his guilt about getting angry with his mother for giving up on life, for being a big burden on him, are in the fore. Again I find myself drifting off, having trouble staying focused on the session material and on Rob himself. I find my mind drifting back to his dream about the bare stone room, and I imagine him sweeping it with a broom. I find I cannot picture the scenery, the backdrop of the Sorcerer's Apprentice scene. I seem to vaguely recall that there's a dream within the cartoon scene itself. I feel stumped and a little frustrated that I cannot remember. I surprise myself by almost interrupting Rob in midsentence: "You said yesterday that one of your thoughts about the dream had to do with the sorcerer's apprentice in *Fantasia*, and I'm wondering what you had in mind."

"Well, I thought the broom in the dream reminded me of it, is what I said. And I guess the scene itself is like in my dream, with the bare, cold-looking stone floor and all."

I decide to follow my instincts. "Isn't there a dream in the story?" I inquire.

Rob looks a bit uncomfortable, perhaps sheepish. "Yeah, remember when Mickey Mouse falls asleep after he teaches the broom to carry the water? He dreams about how powerful he will become, and in his dream he is directing the oceans and the stars as if he were an intergalactic orchestra director. He is very powerful in his dream, but meanwhile he has abdicated all responsibility by falling asleep while the broom does his work. He's using the sorcerer's magical power, and it's a power he doesn't know how to control yet, even though he will know how someday soon.

"He wakes up to find his chair starting to float because the broom has carried so much water into the house. He tries chopping the broom into pieces, but each piece becomes a new broom and begins carrying water, following his original order. The situation gets worse and worse, and he nearly drowns, trying to read the sorcerer's manual to find out what to do. Then the sorcerer wakes up, discovers the flood, and reverses the spell. He is annoyed with Mickey, and Mickey is recalcitrant but also clearly glad to see him. With a swat of the broom, the sorcerer puts Mickey back in his place. He ends up being the sorcerer's apprentice again, taking up his buckets to carry water, uncomplainingly this time." Rob pauses, tentative and apparently uncomfortable on the couch.

"So the sorcerer puts him back in his place?"

"Yes." I wait, allowing the tense silence to crescendo. "I guess you could say that my raising the Prozac on my own, without permission from you, is a little like usurping your power, stealing your thunder." Rob appears to be waiting for a reprimand from me, a swat to put him in his place, perhaps.

The three evolving neural circuits that are of a social and emotional nature allow the child to learn to control and modulate previously uncontrolled emotional displays, as well as to rein in his impulses through both loving and disapproving interactions with his primary caretakers. In addition, experience begins to cause the child to generate expectations of how important others around him are likely to behave based on history. Part of why disapproval is such a blow to the toddler is that he has learned to expect positive, elating caretaker amplifications of his already positive internal state. The child's expectations about how others will behave are natural forerunners to the formation of prototypes.

You also may be beginning to suspect that all these socio-emotional representations have something to do with self-esteem and its regulation. Schore cites a definition of self-esteem in which it is conceptualized as "an affective picture of the self." Thus, high self-esteem connotes a predominance of positive affects, such as elation, in association with one's self-image, while low self-esteem connotes an abundance of negative emotions, such as shame. In fact, effective self-esteem regulation results in a preponderance of positive affects in connection with the sense of self, such as enjoyment and excitement.

If all goes well enough during the development of these three circuits in the first two years of life, then the child can effectively self-regulate the tone and intensity of his emotions in a variety of under- and over-stimulating social environments. He has become an effective regulator of his own internal state.

Of course, many patients in psychotherapy have not learned this self-regulatory ability, and part of what I am trying to do during their treatment is give them a chance to develop a broader affective range as well as an improved capacity to regulate the intensity of their emotional experience for themselves. If you think back to Kandel and his sea slugs, you may wonder, as I do, if I am literally reworking the cortico-limbic connections that were either not formed or not properly formed during their childhood development. While it is hard to prove this in the living human brain, my clinical experience suggests that most patients do indeed gain access to a broader affective range as well as an increased sense that they can effectively regulate their own internal states. In fact, an interesting study by psychotherapy researchers David E. Orlinsky and Jessie D. Geller showed that thoughts about the therapist between sessions occur regularly in about 90 percent of those engaged in psychotherapy in outpatient settings, and that these representations are evoked most vividly at points where the patient is attempting to mitigate painful feelings like sadness, anxiety, depression, and guilt. Indeed, patients seem to evoke the representation of the therapist to "feel less alone, less anxious/depressed, less overwhelmed and more connected." These representations, driven by a desire to modulate painful affects, show the ways in which the therapist and the therapeutic relationship come to make up a patient's mind. In fact, it may be the experiencing of affective states in the context of the intense psychotherapeutic relationship that helps adult patients regain some of the plasticity that they had in toddlerhood—neural flexibility that can help them to change.

I think about how in *Fantasia* the sorcerer's rule over his apprentice is like the rule of a father over a son. The sorcerer puts the apprentice back in his place at the end of the scene, with a gentle yet firm swat to the seat of Mickey's pants with the trouble-causing broom. I find myself thinking about how Rob often was left at home with his mother while his father was away on long business trips, left to function as the de facto man of the house too soon for his own good, before he knew how to handle himself. Wait a minute, I think incredulously. Rob told me that in the dream he wanted to get into bed with his mother, and I ignored it. Surely I usually would have paid more attention to a patient telling me that he wants to get into bed with his mother—even if she might be dead or depressed—than I have just now with Rob. In a flash I see Rob's pecker, which already has gotten under the covers, as the real danger between Rob and his mother. I smile at the idea of a pecker "personified" as a dangerous blackbird.

Rob himself goes further with this theme right away, taking a deep breath and then jumping in. "I feel nervous about admitting it"—he swallows hard—"but yesterday when I left I was noticing your breasts and thinking about putting my head between them, nuzzling you. Then I wondered if you had a husband or a boyfriend that would get mad at me; I imagined him lurking in the waiting room, ready to beat me up. It's embarrassing to talk about."

"Perhaps it's easier to talk about depressed listlessness than sex. After all, you've said before that you looked forward as a boy to getting into bed with your mother while your father was away, that it made you feel excited." I realize that I have unwittingly redirected the conversation back toward Rob's mother, away from myself. Ideally I would have liked to keep the focus on the here and now, on Rob and me, because it makes the issue we are focused on palpable and alive in the room with us rather than more distant, displaced, past history. In fact, probably it is the very intensity of the tension between Rob and me that has led me to take the easier route, looking at Rob's relationship with his mother instead of with me. Rob is making me uncomfortable. As if in response to my discomfort, he follows my lead and returns to talking about his mother.

"The truth is, there were lots of times when I did get in bed with my mother, even when she was depressed, and enjoyed being there. And I had a funny dream last night. I dreamed that the analytic couch here unfolded into a double bed, and it had a bedspread on it. You were going to come and get in with me, and I was feeling panicky but excited, a feeling that was unclear, like am I getting an erection or do I have to pee?" Rob seems suddenly to realize what he has been saying, and pauses, embarrassed.

"What made you stop?" I ask.

"Well, I'm back to the sorcerer's apprentice thing again. I mean, what started as getting a little comfort by cuddling with her in bed got way out of hand, like I didn't know how to handle feeling excited and being close to her. At one point when I was eight or nine, I think she realized I was excited, and she made me get out of bed, saying that my father would be home soon. I guess I got the message that he wouldn't be happy, finding me excited and in bed with her. Just like I feel your boyfriend or husband wouldn't be amused to find me noticing your breasts."

The good thing about making mistakes as a psychotherapist is that patients almost always give you a second chance if you look for it. Rob has brought the issue right back to me. "The danger is that the apprentice will get so caught up in what he's doing, in acting like a sorcerer and in feeling powerful and strong, that the situation can get totally out of hand before he even realizes it. It seems like part of what you're saying is that you feel like your own sexual yearnings threaten to get totally out of hand, both with your mother when you were younger and now with me."

"I was waiting in the dream about the couch for you to come and get into bed with me, but I was scared as well, like I was about to get into trouble."

Silence.

"I'm hoping the session is nearly over because I have the feeling that I need to get out of here."

"It sounds like you're feeling very uncomfortable as we're talking about your yearnings and your excitement. I have the sense that you want to leave to protect me and to protect yourself from the situation getting out of hand. It's as if the crow that lands on the bedcovers and starts trying to peck its way into bed with you and your mother were your desires or your sexuality threatening to get out of control, menacing the cozy comfort of being in bed with your mother. But we do need to stop here for today."

"Now I get the sense that you're kicking me out like my mother did. For a minute I was wondering whether you had another patient after me, or perhaps you're meeting your husband. If I see another man in the waiting room on my way out the door, I'm going to glare at him," Rob remarks in a droll tone. He collects his belongings and turns to smile and wink at me over his shoulder as he leaves.

His wink reminds me again of the Brokaw billboard and I suddenly recall its punchline: "If it ain't Brokaw, fix it." If the Brokaw character on the nightly news is a sexy, strong man who is comfortable with his own power and appeal, Rob ain't Brokaw yet. But he isn't as broken as he sometimes feels, either. His fears of competition, angry retaliation, and sexuality keep him from being like Brokaw, but perhaps in time we'll fix that.

6

The Madonna of
the Prozac Capsule

As I was walking out of the office after the last ses-
sion, I had a funny visual image, like a daydream.
It sounds silly, but what I pictured was your face
superimposed on my Prozac capsule. It was a funny
image, like a Madonna appearing from out of
nowhere on the side of a barn or something. I
thought it meant that you were one part of what
I needed, and Prozac was the other. Almost as if I
was taking you in along with the medicine.

Frances shifts uneasily on the couch, apparently uncomfortable with this expression of needing me. "I
dubbed my visitation the Revelation of Dr. Vaughan
of the Prozac," she says, her tone becoming more playful.
"You're not Catholic, are you?"

I ask Frances what it would mean if I were.

"I knew you would ask me that!" she answers with glee.

"You were right," I rejoin, reminding myself not to let Frances distract me from the daydream image. I marvel for a moment at all the "encapsulated" issues her vision of me and the Prozac together reveals. One is the intensity of her need for a relationship with me; it is just as important as her Prozac, if not more so. After all, I am the one who has given her the medication in the first place. Her amusing image also suggests just how interconnected relationships and pills can be.

When she began therapy, Frances believed that her depressive tendencies were inborn and biological, caused by defective brain chemistry and beyond her control. Her family history amply supported this view. Frances felt sure she needed medication to fix her neurochemistry, and I agreed that she had symptoms of major depressive illness, so over the first months of therapy I started her on Prozac.

But another part of Frances believed just as strongly that she simply needed to snap out of it, that her depression was a self-indulgence that she and I could "talk her out of" if we tried hard enough. If feeling depressed were within her control, then choosing to remain depressed showed that she was just being a bad, morally inferior person. When she held this view, Frances fervently believed that all she needed was psychotherapy to help her overcome her badness, to encourage her to pull herself up by her own bootstraps. If she could just be good enough, strong-willed enough, depression need never overtake her again. In this view, Frances didn't have to acknowledge that she might have an illness that she could not control. Her interest in answering this mind-brain, psychology-biology question was intense, and it was part of what had led her to go back to school to become a psychologist.

Frances's two views of her depression, polar opposites, can be seen as an embodiment of the mind-brain problem within her own mind (and brain). Yet these two views suggest also that the complex role of affect is at the heart of the matter itself. When Frances seems more depressed, is a genetically caused problem in neurotransmitters making her sad, with her sadness temporarily changing her view of herself and others within relationships? Or is a shift in her views of herself or others actually causing the depression? Or both? These are modern psychiatry's (and often our patients') versions of the chicken-and-egg question, so complicated that it is tempting to roast the chicken, make an omelet of the egg, and forget the whole thing.

The evolution of the cortico-limbic circuits I described in the last chapter suggests that there is a complex, highly entwined relationship among a person's capacity to experience a range of positive and negative affects, his self-esteem, his ability to self-regulate both the tone and intensity of emotional states as well as self-esteem, and his early life relationships. In short, Schore's work suggests that our early caretakers are nothing short of very powerful external regulators of our brain's evolving connections and neurochemistry. This model suggests that the quality of the caretaker-child relationship itself is intensely important. In this chapter I examine what we know about the effects of caretaker misattunement and separation on subsequent development. I then show that the problems we would predict and that we see in animal models are indeed common in adults seeking intensive psychotherapy. Finally, I discuss the different roles of psychotherapy and medication.

Several ideas implicit in the cortico-limbic circuitry model of the last chapter suggest what can go wrong in the first two years of life and imply what subsequent problems might result. For instance, a depressed caretaker might be unable to participate in the amplification of the infant's elation in early life. Such a child might later have a limited capacity for the experience and regulation of positive affects, such as elation, and a lack of positive self-esteem.

An overly attached caretaker might be unwilling to rupture, even momentarily, her bond with her child, leading to problems with socialization, poor impulse control, and difficulty with age-appropriate separation. A caretaker who cannot even temporarily disabuse her child of the notion that he is perfect and the center of her universe will tend to make him overly dependent on the praise of others for the regulation of his own self-esteem. He will tend to suffer from what Schore calls "underregulation" disturbances—to be unable to regulate negative affective states.

An overworked, chronically stressed caretaker might be predominantly irritable and angry, viewing the child as another burden on an overly long list. This caretaker might refuse to take the time to repair the relationship with the toddler once it has ruptured. Thus, the caretaker would leave the toddler in a low-arousal state of depression and shame with a negative self-image, perhaps setting the stage for depression and anxiety and the associated feelings of worthlessness and helplessness.

Studies with animals show that early life separation does indeed lead to the results that Schore's cortico-limbic circuitry model predicts. Attachment-researcher Myron Hofer found that even a rat pup responds during the very first episode of separation from the mother with high-pitched calling noises.

Hofer also demonstrated that an isolated pup is extremely motivated to reconnect with its mother and will learn complicated mazes to get back to her; even short periods of contact with the mother act as powerful reinforcers. And even in rats, the effects of maternal separation are dramatic: separation-anxious rats call at rates double those of rat pups who have not experienced separation, when once again separated from their mothers.

Researcher Charles Nemeroff and his colleagues at Emory University showed that maternal separation in both rats and primates causes a stress response with increased production of the hormone cortisol, which in turn causes important growth hormones to plummet. Growth hormone is responsible for a wide range of metabolic activities in the body, and decreasing it can lead to brain changes that may ultimately slow the growth of the evolving cortico-limbic loops, perhaps ultimately setting the tone of the subject's resting state at too high a level of reactivity. In this way, the stress induced by separation may set the stage for depressive and anxiety disorders in later life.

Another study showed that when stressful and unstable feeding conditions that alter the availability of the mother are imposed on monkeys in a colony, the infant monkeys are greatly affected. Leonard A. Rosenblum and his colleagues changed the way food was offered to the three groups of monkeys. There was always enough food available, but the conditions under which the food was obtained differed. One group of monkeys was placed in a low–foraging demand situation, meaning that the mother monkeys did not have to look very hard or for very long to obtain the food they needed. The second group was placed in a high–foraging demand condition, in which food was harder to find, requiring more time and effort on the part of the mother monkeys. The third group was switched between high– and low–foraging demand situations every two weeks.

When foraging demand was stable, whether high or low, the monkeys behaved normally. However, major changes occurred within the monkey colony when foraging conditions switched from high to low. Specifically, there was less mutual grooming and more dominance behavior among the adult monkeys, causing increased tension within the colony. Between mothers and infants there was increased overall contact, but also an increase in the number of times that contact was broken and then reestablished. That is, the mothers repeatedly tried to separate from their infants while the infants struggled to reestablish contact, not unlike a clingy toddler who holds on to his parent's leg as the parent tries to leave for work.

The impact of the separation on the infant monkeys was

pronounced: Play levels fell far below the averages of the monkeys in the stable foraging situation; curiosity and interest in exploration declined; playful interactions with mother and others decreased; and the infants often assumed passive, hunched, depressed-looking positions.

It is noteworthy that the infant monkeys fared well when the mother was subjected to stable foraging conditions, whether high or low foraging was required. Whether the mother searched for food for two hours or for ten, as long as the separation was predictable, the infants developed normally. What really made the infant monkeys anxious was changing unpredictably from one foraging situation to the other, which brought with it unpredictability about how long the separation from the mother would be from day to day. This unpredictability led to mother-infant interactions that were characterized by clinginess on the part of the infants and annoyed attempts to separate on the part of the mothers.

Two short-term studies by Stern suggest that even in the absence of physical separation, lack of maternal attentiveness and responsivity has a marked impact on human infants. In the first study, Stern and his colleagues watched a videotape of a mother and child playing together, and showed the mother the examples of attunement that they found. They then asked the mother to deliberately misattune herself to the child. For instance, under normal conditions, a mother might jiggle her son's bottom in rhythm with his excited arm-flailing as he encounters a new toy. Researchers would ask her instead to jiggle his bottom at a faster or slower rate than his arm movements, to be out of sync. When the mother jiggled the tot's bottom in rhythm with his arm flailing, the child did not look at her and continued to play. But when she made her jiggling overly fast or slow, the baby looked quizzically at her, as if to inquire, "What's up?" He seemed to experience the misattunement as an indication that something was wrong.

In another fascinating study, mothers without histories of anxiety or depression were asked by Stern and his colleagues to suddenly become "stonefaced," that is, not to respond to their young infants. When they did, their babies cried, then made various cooing efforts to reengage their mothers, and finally seemed listless and dejected, with greatly reduced vocalizations and movements. So profound was this short-term effect on the infants that many mothers in the study found it too upsetting, even impossible, to maintain the stony appearance even for several minutes. They often "gave in," responding to the infant's distress by breaking into smiles or cooing. I sometimes remember this study at moments in psychotherapy when I "give in" and laugh at a patient's joke or answer her question.

There is good evidence to suggest also that early life separation produces long-term consequences. In Hofer's studies, rat pups with histories of separations continued to have distress calls—calls for help to their mothers—into adolescence and adulthood, whereas rat pups without separation in early life cease their distress calls in infancy. So effective is the separation paradigm in the generation of anxiety that researchers use separation to produce anxious rats on whom to test new antianxiety drugs!

In another project, litters of rat pups were removed en

The Madonna of the Prozac Capsule

masse from their home cages for three hours daily during the first two weeks of life. They remained in another cage together with their littermates, and received adequate nutrition and warmth while away from Mama Rat. Researchers tested these rat pups after they reached adulthood by placing them in an empty cage in which Cocoa Crispies (which apparently are ambrosia to rats) were hidden under wood chips. The rats were allowed to roam around freely in the cage, exploring and searching for the treats, but there was one small enclosed place in the cage in which the rats could hide.

Rats with no history of maternal separation homed in on the Cocoa Crispies immediately, while rats who had histories of maternal deprivation cowered in the enclosed area, venturing out to explore very little, thereby forfeiting the chance for Cocoa Crispies treats. In the monkey colonies also, the infants whose mothers had experienced the changing foraging situations also responded as if they too were chronically anxious.

By now you must be feeling as tense as I did when I first read about these studies. I spent a good fifteen minutes trying to think of ways to take three years off from work to raise my children. But then I began to realize that if a rat lives two years and a person lives eighty, a three-hour separation for a rat pup is like a five-day (120-hour) separation for an infant. Considering also the monkey studies I described earlier (in which a cloth-covered mother and a normal peer were good enough for normal development to take place), you may want to think twice about giving up your career. While everyone wants their children to get all the Cocoa Crispies out of life that they can, we also must keep in mind that mother rats aren't expected to go to law school, read Dr. Spock, or even visit Bloomingdale's. More studies are needed to show us the effects of maternal separation on children. Separation and deprivation are not necessarily the same.

Still, many studies—including one recent study of patients in psychoanalysis—have shown that the connection between early life loss, abandonment, abuse, and neglect and later problems with mood and anxiety disorders, self-esteem, and interpersonal relationships is a strong one. When Norman Doidge and his colleagues in Toronto surveyed psychiatrists about the childhood histories of patients in psychoanalysis, they found that of the 580 patients described, 23 percent had experienced traumatic separations, 23 percent spontaneously reported sexual abuse, 22 percent had been physically abused, and 21 percent had a parent or sibling die when they were an average age of ten. This provides evidence for the clinical observation that patients who seek intensive psychotherapy often have a substantial history of childhood loss, separation, neglect, or abuse. The patients in Doidge's study had high rates of mood disorders (found in 65 percent), anxiety disorders (49 percent), sexual dysfunction (43 percent) and substance abuse (12 percent).

My own research—performed at the Columbia Center for Psychoanalytic Training and Research in New York City in collaboration with Drs. Steven Roose, Randall Marshall, Roger MacKinnon, and Lisa Mellman—reveals that disorders of mood and anxiety comprise the vast majority of diagnoses among patients seeking psychodynamic treatment.

In fact, fully half of those beginning treatment at our center have a current major depressive episode, typified by symptoms of sleep and appetite disturbance, depressed mood, loss of capacity for pleasure, hopelessness, and suicidal thoughts. Our work, taken together with Doidge's findings, suggests that people seeking long-term treatment often have the very histories of trauma, childhood separations and losses, and subsequent depressive and anxiety disorders that our cortico-limbic circuitry model predicts.

What can make us go for the Cocoa Crispies in life after a history of separation that makes us chronically anxious and depressed? You may find it surprising that I have gotten to this point in my argument with nary a word about Prozac. After all, antidepressant and antianxiety medications are as common in our culture as McDonald's; Prozac alone boasts, "Over 40 million served." But it was necessary first to explain how complicated the interplay is between early life relationships, positive and negative affects, and the regulation of emotions and self-esteem, and only then to explain how I think medication fits into that picture.

Paxil, the third medicine in the Prozac dynasty, caused our cowering rats to find their courage; when they were given Paxil, they searched for the cereal as enthusiastically as the other rats without separation histories. But when the Paxil was stopped, they returned to cowering behind the bunkers once again. It is fascinating that a medication could go such a long way toward correcting a behavior, such as anxious cowering, that arose from early childhood separation. This fact was the leitmotif of Peter Kramer's *Listening to Prozac*. But my patients and I find it frustrating when the effects that they achieved on medication vanish when they stop it. After the initial hoopla about the effectiveness of Prozac passes, many patients whose chronic depressive and anxiety symptoms are much improved through medication are grateful for how much better they feel, yet they are left wondering, "Am I supposed to take this stuff forever?"

And even though sometimes taking medication and feeling better can help people feel quite different and can allow them to make impressive strides on their own to change themselves and their lives, often such change is either totally terrifying to patients and results in their stopping the medication, or not enough for them to really change their lives. For most people, medication changes how they feel, but psychotherapy is what changes what their lives are like. After all, an often neglected fact about the patients in *Listening to Prozac* is that they all were in long-term, relatively intensive psychotherapies.

Highlighting the complicated links among relationships, separation, neurotransmitters, and chronic depressive and anxiety symptoms, other studies suggest that the therapeutic relationship itself actually can produce results similar to those obtained with medications like Prozac, bolstering a patient's depressed mood or quelling his anxiety. In one study, patients with significant depressive symptoms felt markedly better after calling to schedule an appointment with a psychiatrist. In fact, this effect is so pronounced that those on placebo medicines in clinical trials of new drugs cause problems for the researchers because they often form enough of a bond with the research assistant who doles out their dummy pills to derive therapeutic benefit from the relationship itself. As with medications, the "antidepressant" effect produced by the contact with an interested other tends to fade rather quickly when the relationship ceases. It is fascinating, but in keeping with the maternal regulation of cortico-limbic structures, that the promise of help through human contact can immediately and positively affect your mood.

Clinical observation also suggests that a depressed or anxious patient engaged in psychotherapy often can feel immensely better on hearing his or her therapist's voice over the phone, or even on the therapist's answering machine. It is not uncommon for a patient who is depressed or anxious to call his therapist's answering machine repeatedly just to hear the therapist's voice. And a comment from the therapist that places the patient's current concerns in the context of her other representations of herself and the world often seems to act like a powerful drug in calming or cheering an anxious or depressed patient.

Generally, medications such as Prozac work by changing the availability of neurotransmitters, which are produced by deep brain centers whose neurons send projections to various parts of the cortex. Medicines may increase the amount of neurotransmitter produced or prolong its action by preventing its breakdown. The deep brain nuclei set the tone or climate of the whole cerebral cortex by messily spritzing their chemicals around, bathing the cortical neurons to create a kind of operating atmosphere for the cortex itself. The presence or absence of important others may also affect the deep brain nuclei directly, altering the type of climate these neurons create. It is possible also that the presence of genes, or a history of early life experiences that predisposes a person to depressive illness, alters the operating climate that the deep nuclei provide for the cortex.

When patients have anxiety or depression, these powerful affects color the story the story synthesizer tells. Like brightness or sharpness on a television set, the affects change the appearance of the overall picture.

When depressive symptoms are produced by a drastic change in the deep nuclei of the cortex, medication may be required to restore the cortical climate to normal. And being depressed and anxious certainly may make psychotherapy harder.

A study my colleagues and I conducted at Columbia looked at the impact of depression on patients' capacity for thinking about the psychological motivations of themselves and others. Patients with a high number of depressive and anxiety symptoms were less capable of this type of thinking, which is essential in psychotherapy, than patients who were less depressed and anxious.

In addition, patients who were more depressed had a sense of agency that was more external. In other words, they tended to believe that bad things just happened to them and that they could do little to change the course of their lives or relationships. Of course, it is difficult for psychotherapy to make an impact on someone who is so depressed that he sees his own behavior as largely irrelevant to what happens in his life. This finding contradicts the idea that painful symptoms such as depression motivate patients for psychotherapeutic treatment, suggesting instead that these symptoms might actually (and, I believe, not surprisingly) get in the way.

We saw in chapter 2 that psychotherapy, like other forms of learning, works probably by changing the connections between cortical neurons themselves. But this process would not be enough by itself to explain why the voice of a stranger on the phone can cheer the depressed patient up; this effect cannot be the result of long-term structural change to the brain. It seems likely that human contact stimulates the cortico-limbic circuits that develop in early life; that positive emotional and physical contact with another human being probably ultimately affects the limbic system as do medicines like Prozac. The operating environment of the cortex undoubtedly is affected by the climate produced by the deep brain nuclei themselves, whether the nuclei are responding to medicine or to a psychotherapeutic relationship, and changing this climate may change how the cortex functions, even if the cortical structure remains the same.

It appears that when the climate change is short-lived, as, for example, when a patient has an episode of depression of a few weeks' to months' duration, the cortex may function differently but maintain its usual structure. However, when the diminished serotonin or norepinephrine production of a patient's deep nuclei becomes chronic, the cortical structure itself ultimately changes. Whether because of a biochemical or genetic problem in the neurons, or because of current or early life loss of relationships that leave their mark on these neurons, the deep nuclei do affect the cortex. (There is even new evidence that the story is not quite in yet on the role of medications in spurring brain development. One new study found that medicines like Prozac that increase serotonin lead to increased amounts of CREB, a nerve protein that causes the growth of new neural connections. This finding suggests that Prozac could help promote the kind of structural brain changes that occur in psychotherapy. Thus, the links are likely to get more complicated than they already are.)

Frances, searching in our therapy for some understanding of her depression, was trying to find a way to synthesize the effects of medication and human contact on the brain. As I sometimes do when a patient is struggling with a mind-body problem, I explained to Frances what I thought her Prozac did, how changes in the climate produced by the deep brain nuclei affect the operation and structure of the cortex.

Imagine a city which gets its water supply from a well deep underground. The layout of the city is analogous to the structure of the upper brain. A series of pipes connect the terrain above to the water below. These pipes are like the deep brain nuclei that produce neurotransmitters and pump them up to the upper layer of the brain. Now imagine that due to a problem down below, the city aboveground gets only half of its usual water. The hundreds of individual homes and businesses above must operate on half the water they are used to receiving. All the homes and businesses above are affected by the problem below, but they are not affected equally. Instead the drought has greater or lesser effects on the individual homes and businesses depending upon how much water they need. The car wash and the Laundromat in the city are obviously in serious trouble, while other businesses like the pizzeria are less affected. The pizzeria can offer their customers beer or soda instead of water. Although the changes in the well of water below affect how life on the surface operates, in the short term they do not change the map of the city itself; the grocery store is still across from the movie theater, whether there's a drought or not.

As the drought continues, the city above will have to begin to shift and change; the car wash will go out of business and be replaced by another business that doesn't need so much water. The same may be true in the brain; if neurotransmitter shortages continue for long enough, they may leave their imprint on the structure of the upper networks of neurons that are responsible for representing the self and important others, just as the desert climate defines what plants can flourish there.

You may be wondering, as Frances sometimes did, why we have not found medications that effectively regulate the upper cortex just as we have found antidepressants that regulate the lower brain nuclei. After all, if we could get a medicine to regulate the upper brain, perhaps we could circumvent the need for psychotherapy. In fact, we have found medications that affect the functioning of the cortical networks, which use primarily the neurotransmitter glutamate.

However, these networks don't respond to medication the way the deep brain does, because the nature of their neural connections is different. The deep brain projections that furnish neurotransmitters to establish the climate of the cortical neural networks tend to spray the neurotransmitter from their synapses rather indiscriminately in a general area of the brain. In this way the deep brain neurons affect many neurons in the neighborhood, like a teenager blasting his music from a boom box on the street, setting the tone or climate of the block. In contrast, the upper cortical neurons are connected to one another by a very tight interconnection, so that the neurotransmitter of the sender affects only the neuron it means to reach. Thus, the upper cortical network neurons each tend to communicate directly with another specific neuron in a very discrete manner, a method more reminiscent of a telephone than a boom box.

This system allows virtually all the cortical neurons we are interested in to use the same excitatory neurotransmitter, glutamate, to communicate. Again the telephone system is a good analogy; it is the establishment of discrete connections, based on different telephone numbers, that enables millions of people to use the same types of digital signals traveling over the same telephone lines to communicate. When the connections in the system are separate, you can use your digital bits to call your mother while ET uses his bits to phone home without getting the messages crossed.

Though changing the neurotransmitters of the upper brain network sounds appealing, when glutamate transmission is manipulated with medicine, so many different cortical cells performing different functions are affected that massive scrambling of the information processing within the cortical networks results. Medication cannot now, and perhaps never will, be able to change problematic patterns of thinking and behaving that are embedded in the upper cortical networks. Instead, the way in which neurons in the upper cortical networks are linked to one another must be changed one by one, a task accomplished only by psychotherapy.

Though providing water—whether in the form of Prozac or human contact—is very helpful to a patient like Frances who grew up in a drought, teaching her how to get or even make water for herself is the ultimate goal of treatment. It is the psychotherapeutic equivalent of teaching her to fish as opposed to simply providing her dinner. We have seen how the effects of the psychotherapeutic relationship and of medications such as Prozac in patients with chronic depression and anxiety are dependent on continued treatment; they can work quite effectively, but their results tend to last only as long as the relationship or the pill supply lasts. The vast majority of patients who want to be free of their mild to moderate depressive and anxiety symptoms don't want to be in psychotherapy or to take medication forever. Do they have a choice?

Often, the answer to this question is yes. In fact, Frances's image of me and Prozac together in the capsule reveals something about how patients can use psychotherapy to achieve a reduction of depressive and anxiety symptoms that persists after treatment ends. Frances's image suggests the growth of a *new* representation within her mind and brain, in which her relationship with me is essential, in which she *is* taking me in along with her Prozac every day. But just what would "taking me in" mean, and how would it help to rid Frances of her depressive symptoms?

One of the ways her emotionally barren childhood affected Frances was that she became overly self-reliant. And in fact, for much of her first two years in psychotherapy, Frances believed that she felt better only because of the Prozac, not because of her relationship with me or because of the things we talked about. Though initially feeling grateful and lucky to find her chronic depressive symptoms assuaged by the pill I had prescribed, Frances soon began to complain bitterly about feeling lonely and empty on the weekends. When I raised the possibility that she was missing me and our sessions, she became angry and upset. Her response was to demand more and more Prozac, even though she also wondered whether she was attempting to control me and worried about whether I was letting her get "addicted" to the medicine or letting her have her way because I was not strong enough to stand up to her. Taking Prozac from me had once been a positive and intimate act, as if Frances were ingesting pieces of our relationship in an encapsulated form. Though she had initially joked about the medicine, crooning "I've got Prozac under my skin," over time she became more and more aware that the Prozac she was taking came from me. Of course she could probably get it from another source, from her internist or even from a friend who took the medication also. But she wanted *my* Prozac, an idea that made her uncomfortable. Having Prozac in her veins was one thing, but the idea that *I* was under her skin was quite another.

Frances's life was altered by Prozac in several regards. She felt happier, more proactive, and more self-confident than ever before. But she was disappointed to find that she still could not form meaningful relationships with others. She tended to find it unnerving when another person had a positive effect on her. She felt thrown off-kilter. When she was free of any attachments, she felt powerful and strong, but relationships quickly made her feel weak and under the sway of strong needs and feelings. Gradually, as Frances became more trusting, and as I did not die or abandon her, she began to acknowledge that our relationship in fact had a profound effect on her, one with which she was not always comfortable.

What Frances did next was surprising. She quite unexpectedly discontinued her Prozac without telling me and once again became more depressed and distant. We explored the meaning of stopping a medicine that had been quite helpful to her, and the degree to which her depressive symptoms kept her tied—albeit in a distressing way—to her depressed, listless mother became more clear. Thus, in addition to her medication functioning as a symbol of her relationship with me, her depressive symptoms served to keep her connected and attached to her mother.

And another meaning emerged in therapy about Frances's decision to stop her medicine. She believed she was getting too well and that getting too well might mean ending therapy or becoming more competitive and clashing more with me. Stopping Prozac and getting depressed seemed the all-around safest solution, a way for Frances to keep me and her mother with her. But I am not under Frances's skin just in the form of Prozac I have prescribed. A representation of me and my relationship with Frances is being literally woven into her mind. This process of internalization of a new relationship has been described by analysts Jerome L. Singer and Kenneth S. Pope as follows:

> *Psychoanalysts often notice that patients in a sense adopt the therapist as a kind of imaginary companion, someone to whom they talk privately in their minds. . . . This pattern of behavior need not be viewed necessarily as an instance of excessive attachment or dependency. Often it is a natural phase of a new learning procedure in which the patient is gradually assimilating what in effect the analyst has been teaching her about a process of self-examination and heightened self-awareness.*

You may recall the study that showed that patients use visual images of their therapists to mitigate painful affective states. Singer and Pope suggest that in taking the therapist in, the patient also gains a new internal friend, what analysts call an imago, which literally changes her mind.

Frances's vision of Prozac and me together marked a turning point in her treatment. Her thoughts about the humorous picture of me on the Prozac pill led her to speculate that though I was not actually with her during the weekends, an internal representation of me, along with the medicine I had prescribed, was indeed present in an enduring way. She began to recognize that she could conjure me up at will to combat her feelings of lonely isolation or social discomfort. She began to grow more comfortable with the idea that her connection to me was very important to her. In allowing herself literally to see my importance to her, Frances felt freer to admit to herself how much other relationships mattered to her as well.

As the time approached when she was ready to stop psychoanalysis with me, Frances recognized more clearly that she now carried me inside. She could stop psychotherapy with me, yet still have me with her. When she ended treatment, she took with her a part of me that had become represented and elaborated in her own neural networks. Her picture of me had become a part of herself she could rely on, an image she could invoke whenever she felt troubled or alone. And the affective connection we had formed also was available to her whenever she needed it, a feeling-representation of our time together that she could evoke at will.

Through the process of psychotherapy, Frances learned what she seemed to have failed to learn from her early life experience with a depressed mother. Her capacity for intense positive and negative emotions, her sense that neither fantasy nor emotion could overwhelm her, meant she was ready to end therapy with me. Once I was truly under her skin, once our relationship, with its affect-regulating function, was encoded in her brain's cortico-limbic system through the slow alteration of connections between neurons, she could gain control over the troubling emotional states she previously had experienced. And though psychoanalysis sometimes has been unfairly viewed as a form of personality plastic surgery for the "worried well," for Frances, as for so many patients, psychoanalysis was not just skin deep. And in Frances's case, psychoanalysis allowed her good enough affective control that she no longer required medication. Though this certainly is not the case for all depressed patients who undergo intensive psychodynamic treatment, ultimately psychoanalysis gave Frances a new vision of herself that was both more magical and more real than the Madonna of the Prozac capsule, me.

7

Whose Story Is It, Anyway?

I was encouraging Helen, my boss at work, to order a bacon, lettuce, and tomato sandwich for lunch, and I was doing the same myself. Somehow I knew it was the first BLT she would ever eat, perhaps because she was Jewish. I felt certain somehow that she and I would spend the afternoon together and then have a second BLT for dinner.

Lee is a bright young Jewish woman, a fiction writer who entered my office for the first time about three years before the dream of the BLT. She was struggling to get her master of fine arts degree so that she could teach creative writing at a high school or college level while pursuing a career as a novelist. That way, she reasoned, she would have uninterrupted summertime breaks in which to write.

She imagined herself ensconced in an airy beach house on North Carolina's Outer Banks, a place she recalled fondly from her childhood, free from responsibility, running on the beach every morning, immersed in her writing all day, then enjoying a glass of wine and the sunset in the evenings. To me it sounded like a distressingly unpeopled life, but to Lee it was a daydream in which she felt powerful and productive.

"I feel puzzled and a little embarrassed about the BLTs, and I'm wondering if they're tempting because they are too salty, too fattening, have too much mayo. They're a very 'un-PC' food for a Jew, even a nonreligious one. It reminds me of that scene in *Annie Hall* where Diane Keaton orders pastrami on white bread with mayonnaise, you know, a sandwich that doesn't fit in for a girl who doesn't belong to the New York deli culture. I guess a BLT is a 'slurpy' kind of sandwich. It makes a mess, but it's also juicy and tempting. You know, of course, that I never would have eaten the BLT in real life." Lee continues, protesting that the funny thing is that BLT's don't even tempt her that much. In fact, she is a vegetarian and an inveterate runner who is dedicated to lean, clean living. "I felt unsettled in the dream, shy and a little overwhelmed about having lunch and dinner with Helen, but I was also really excited to get to spend the day with her. She's an example of an attractive, successful career woman."

Hearing Lee describe her boss as attractive reminds me that Lee has speculated on several occasions about whether or not her supervisor is a lesbian, a thought that prompts my next remark. "So it was like a long date with her, an afternoon sandwiched between the two BLTs?" I ask. Lee and I have already established that she remembers feeling attracted to women since she was five or six, but she "decided" during college that she was heterosexual. She dated with a vengeance, determined to find herself a husband and to block out of her mind the thoughts she had about other women.

Lee groans as she makes her first conscious connection between lesbianism and the BLT. "Ugh—are you trying to tell me that my supervisor, like the BLT, is forbidden, something I crave, something that I am not supposed to want or feel drawn to, but secretly I do?" I remain silent, quite sure that Lee knows by now that these words are hers, not mine.

"I'm leaving that alone for now," Lee says. "I'm putting you on notice that I'm changing tacks. I was wondering what about the bacon itself, why it's a BLT and not some other more 'kosher' sandwich. I'm thinking about the Jewish-pork connection. Pork, I mean pigs, are a funny thing. They're so cute when they're baby piglets, with their pink ears, and they're cuddly. They have perfect translucent skin and soft hair."

I find myself puzzled about how Lee, born and bred in New York, has gotten so close to a piglet, so I ask her, "How did you have occasion to play with piglets?"

"I saw them when my friend Pam and I were at her uncle's farm. She and her family had the beach house next to mine in Nags Head. One weekend I went with her to visit her uncle, and I remember he brought baby piglets up to the house the morning they were born and let us play with them. We played house, and they were our babies to feed and change for the day. Then her uncle took them back and rolled them around in some dirt by the barn to get our smell off them, so their mother would take them back. We watched as he put them back with their mother, and I felt so sad."

"What seemed sad to you at the time?" I asked Lee.

"I think it was the idea that they were going to be killed when they got older. I remember wishing that they would be like Wilbur, the pig in *Charlotte's Web*. I wished they would find a way to seem miraculously talented, to be "some pig," and then her uncle would let them live, not take them to slaughter. They seemed so different from the hogs we saw being taken to market that summer, these big truckloads full of smelly, dirty pigs headed to market. And it was unthinkable to imagine these cute little piglets hog-tied, hanging by their back legs from the trees." Lee shudders.

"And yet you thought about it . . ." I let my voice trail off, trying not to sound accusatory or judgmental.

"I ate the BLT, didn't I?" Lee responds. "At least in my dream I did." She laughs nervously, but then there is a shift as she begins to take ownership of the images, begins to sketch childhood memories, inner fantasies. I imagine that she is at a writing class, furiously outlining a new idea for a chapter in her novel, with enough time only to capture the main shapes of the story as it is appearing in her mind's eye. She now speaks with urgency and purpose, creating a verbal mosaic of images, thoughts, and smells: the gaping slit that ran up the hogs' bellies as they hung in the trees; the acrid smell of burning hog bristles as they were blowtorched off the hogs' skin; the parts of the pigs that weren't recognizable and those that were; the whole bloody carnage being sorted by hefty, industrious, red-faced families who looked a bit piggy themselves.

I begin to feel nauseated, and I notice my palms are damp. Ordinarily in such circumstances I'd be feeling more interested about why I'm getting nauseated, but my thoughts about the hogs and the BLT are so graphic and are making me feel so ill that my curiosity doesn't stand a chance against them. Partly because I cannot overcome my queasiness, I decide to interrupt. Not a very good reason for a comment, but I have the feeling that if I don't intervene, I may have to excuse myself from the session in a minute. "So what do you think is the connection between dining on these BLTs with Helen in your dream and thinking now about the piglets and the slaughtering of the hogs you saw with Pam?" Pretty general as a question, but an efficient way to take a moment's breather from the hog onslaught.

"Well, you and I have talked about how in a way Pam was my first love. I remember feeling it was so nice playing house with her. It was compelling, you know, the idea of having children and a home with her. Once we talked about having a really cool home in California together. It was when we were in about seventh grade. We loved halter tops and jeans at the time, and we even mapped out a whole bedroom for ourselves with drawers dedicated only to jeans and halter tops. It was like we would be out from under our parents and could do anything we wanted. We even used to talk about having babies together. She was squeamish about being pregnant and scared of the pain of being in labor. But I wasn't put off by all that, it was just that I couldn't see myself as a mother. I felt that I didn't have it in me. I didn't even like dolls, except Barbies, because they weren't baby dolls. They were grown-up women with real breasts, and I used to make them fool around with each other." Lee laughs, but she seems to have returned to the subject she warned me she was leaving before.

"I think that summer was the first time that I had the idea that when I was older things would get ugly, just like they did with the pigs. They were cute and innocent as babies, but when they matured, they were horrible, monstrous, and flabby creatures. They were dangerous, too, with little snapping teeth, if you came in their pens." I find myself jarred by this last image and I wonder if pigs do indeed have teeth. I have no idea whether they do or not.

If I've managed to convey only one thing in this neurobiological romp through the brain and mind, I hope it's how important and central I believe the stories of our lives really are. Lee's is a story of forbidden desires and appetites, about being small and lovable or big and disgusting, a demure little girl or an autonomous sexual woman. Like all powerful stories, it is packed with symbols, layers of meaning nested within one another. The BLT might somehow symbolize lesbianism, but it also interdigitates in important ways with Lee's feelings about being Jewish. Hearing the dream and her associations to it, you can almost see her cortical networks as they crank out the narrative of her dream just as they construct the story of her life. As Ethel Person notes in her recent book, *By Force of Fantasy*, the inner theater of the mind is one in which we are simultaneously author, player, and audience.

Whose Story Is It, Anyway?

Stories are the currency of the psychotherapeutic endeavor. They are thoroughly inescapable. Researchers Lester Luborsky, Paul Crits-Christoph, and their colleagues at the University of Pennsylvania found four stories per hour in the sessions of patients in the first year of weekly therapy. Like the abundance of affective attunements between parent and child, the ubiquity of narratives in psychotherapy sessions suggests that they serve some important function, comprising an important form of communication between patient and analyst.

But beyond the psychotherapy research suggesting that telling stories helps us get better in therapy, the value of understanding our life story is simply that it is *our* life story. It captures something key about who we are and how we came to be. With self-understanding comes autonomy. The story of your life is something you will always have, something that defines you. No one can take it away.

Psychoanalyst Roy Schafer has argued that psychoanalysis derives its therapeutic power specifically through the "retelling of a life" that takes place. This retelling ultimately allows us to synthesize a cohesive life narrative. It makes our history make sense, transforms it from a series of unintegrated fragments of plots into a magnum opus. In providing us with an opportunity to integrate disparate elements of our autobiographies, all depth therapies such as psychoanalysis allow us to conquer the past and move toward the future with a new sense of mastery.

But if the story synthesizer located in our cortex is of such fundamental importance in our lives, why don't we see the

stories it concocts with more clarity? If stories are so important, why are they so opaque? After all, most of us love stories, and few have difficulty following the plotline of a movie
or discerning its symbols and the motives of its characters.
So why should our own stories be different?

The traditional psychodynamic explanation for why it is
that we cannot see the stories of our lives is that the protagonist—each one of us—has unacceptable motives and
wishes that the workings of our minds help to guard us from
seeing. The Freudian model of the mind presumes the existence of the dynamic unconscious. The idea of the dynamic unconscious is that our aggressive and sexual drives
press for expression, and they are tenuously held in check by
equally strong counterforces, the defense mechanisms that
struggle to keep the aggressive and sexual drives out of conscious awareness. Thus we are inherently in dynamic conflict, buffeted by our unconscious wishes on the one hand,
and by the constraints of what is acceptable to us on the
other.

Freud believed that our sexual and aggressive wishes are
the natural longings of the Beast Within, a legacy of our animal past that is antithetical to the requirements of a civilized
society and therefore potentially dangerous. Indeed, the importance with which sex and aggression are viewed as motivators of human behavior by psychoanalysts is captured by
the saying, "Everything is about sex, except sex, which is
about aggression." I think of the Beast Within as a wolf, perhaps the wolf from the story of Little Red Riding Hood.
Like the wolf dressed up as Grandma, our inner wishes and

fantasies about others hide effectively—though not completely—from our awareness. The process of psychotherapy, then, is partly a process of looking for those places where the fur sticks out from under Grandma's nightie.

I probably picked the wolf to be the Beast Within because it is such a common childhood experience to worry about the wolf hiding under the bed or in the closet. As children, we were relieved when we finally got the nerve to turn the lights on and found that no wolf was there. We were quite correct to be scared of wolves growing up, but we were looking in the wrong place for the wolf that frightened us. Because when the lights come on in psychotherapy, the wolf we confront is the Wolf Within.

You may be amused by the idea of our Inner Wolf (so much more interesting than having an Inner Child, don't you think?). But you also may be wondering why I've encouraged you throughout this book to tackle some difficult science and showed you what happens to the brain in psychotherapy. And now here I am telling you a Freudian Fairy Tale. But there is evidence that there are ideas and conflicts we just don't want to see.

You may recall from chapter 1 that psychotherapy-researcher Lester Luborsky and his colleagues assembled a wide array of stories from various individuals by searching psychotherapy session transcripts, asking people to recount their dreams and the stories of relationships past and present, and asking people to make up fictional stories. One of the advantages of Luborsky's system—looking for the wish of the story's protagonist, the response of the other character(s), and the subsequent response of the protagonist—is that it breaks stories up into the sparest of outlines. And time and again these bare-bones versions of the stories of our lives contain the same conflicts, the one or two most typical of us. In fact, conflict was such an important component of the stories of our lives that Luborsky termed his method the Core Conflictual Relationship Theme Method, or CCRT.

In a fascinating study, researchers Howard Shevrin and James S. Bond summarized the narrative themes they found, using Luborsky's method, in the initial interviews of patients beginning psychodynamic psychotherapy. The researchers then chose key, conflict-laden words or phrases that hinted at the core themes they had discovered in the stories of each patient. They entered these key words or phrases in a computer and asked each patient to perform the following task. The researchers flashed the key words derived from the patient's own narratives, as well as words derived from the narratives of other patients, on the computer screen and asked each subject to read aloud what the screen said.

The words were shown for two different amounts of time. In one case, the words were shown for too short an amount of time to be identified by the subjects (a perception known as subliminal, or below the threshold for consciousness). In the other case, words were shown for a long enough time to be identified by the patients (supraliminally, or above the threshold for conscious perception). When the words were conflict-laden key words drawn from their own narratives, the subjects could correctly repeat them only when they were shown subliminally, and not supraliminally. In other words, the patients actually did *better* at identifying words that were conflict-laden for them when they saw them for a shorter time. They did much worse when they saw the words for a longer time. Of course, this runs counter to what we would expect. Normally, the longer you see the word or phrase, the better your chance of reading it correctly. And in fact, when patients were shown words that were conflict-laden for others but not for themselves, they did better when they saw the words for longer.

The researchers argued that when stimuli were shown very briefly, they did not reach the cortical level, the point at which they could be consciously identified. They were processed only in subcortical locations—what Freud called the unconscious. In contrast, when the words were shown for longer, the processing of the word reached the level of the cortex, where barriers to its proper recognition were erected, presumably because it evoked anxiety by its sexual or aggressive content. In other words, the more important—and revealing of their conflict-laden wishes and needs—the words shown to the subjects were, the less likely they were to see them. Perhaps this reluctance to see things that would trouble us makes sense, protecting us from painful affects like anxiety and depression. Defenses also play a role in our ability to modulate and contain overwhelming affects.

Of course, to justify one of the main premises of Freud's model of the mind on the basis of one study is far from scientifically acceptable. But studying the unconscious is like studying the wind; its presence must be inferred. And the Wolf Within is like the wind in the sails of our stories, providing a source of power, energy, and vitality that pushes the narratives forward.

While I am focused on the question of whether pigs have teeth without quite knowing why it matters, Lee's Inner Wolf continues to push her thoughts in a direction she was hoping to avoid.

"In a funny way, I can't get away from your earlier comment even though I want to, because there *is* something about the BLTs that I imagine might be similar to having sex with a woman."

"What'd you have in mind?"

"I don't know, I guess it might be kind of salty, or maybe juicy. It's making me sick to think about it."

"It's far from an entirely pleasant idea."

"Yeah, it's intriguing and grotesque at the same time. It's a secret craving that ought to remain secret because I should be ashamed of it. I am ashamed of it, but I can't help but feel drawn to it as well. It doesn't go along with my image to be stuffing down BLTs. And it doesn't go along with my identity to be a lesbian."

"So I'm permitting you or even encouraging you to do something self-destructive?"

Silence.

"I'm recalling that what you were allowed to eat was a point of contention with your mother when you were younger, too," I remind Lee.

"Yep, I had a prototypical Jewish mother, I guess, encouraging me to eat, eat, eat, and then fretting if she thought

I was too fat. Talking about this is making me remember that phrase 'You can't make a silk purse out of a sow's ear.' In a sense I think she saw being Jewish and female as being a sow's ear, not that desirable and certainly not a silk purse. She kind of worshiped women who were the height of WASPishness, who had those blonde fine straight locks as opposed to her unruly, curly, Jewish hair.

"I guess ever since I started developing as a woman I've been feeling more like a sow's ear than a silk purse myself. But with me it's somehow all tied up with my feelings about being attracted to other women. I guess it always seems like they're the real women, the feminine ones, while I play second fiddle. It's like I'm a less appealing sort of a woman myself.

"My mother always comments if I don't wear the right jewelry or if my purse doesn't match my shoes, that sort of thing. And I feel like, Who cares? Who has the time to worry about that kind of thing? I'm too busy with my writing and with school to pay attention. But then again it does bother me when she comments on things like that. I guess it makes me feel masculine, in the stereotypical sense of rough, coarse, unpolished, boorish."

"It seems you feel piggish, like your appetites, including your appetite for other women, are bad and grotesque. Connected with feeling piggish is a sense of being less of a woman, not a genuine woman, more like a sow's ear, something that can never become a silk purse. But in your dream, Helen is tempted by you into eating a BLT, something she's never done before. And she likes it, likes it enough to want to spend the afternoon with you."

"It's much harder for me to have sex with women than with men. I care a lot more what other women think. The stakes are higher. I guess it feels like women are more aware of what I'm supposed to be and whether or not I look like I should. I feel simultaneously competitive with them and in awe of them, almost like a little sister looking up to them. Like gawky Skipper next to Baywatch Barbie. I'm afraid if I were really to have a relationship with a woman I'd always feel inferior to them. Whereas with men I'm on top because their appetite is bigger than mine. They're like animals."

"In other words, when you're with a man, he's the pig but if you were with a woman, you'd be the pig?"

"Yeah, with women I'm the sow's ear and they're the silk purse."

"If your desire makes you a pig, what do you think about Helen devouring the BLT and liking it, too?"

"It feels like I made her do it, that it's not something she'd do on her own."

"You seduced her into it?"

"Yes. And it's something she'll ultimately be mad at me about, like encouraging a friend to break her diet. But because I forced her into it she's kind of absolved of any responsibility for it. So she doesn't need to feel bad or guilty. Her appetite's not really at fault." Lee sighs.

After following Lee's train of thoughts, you may find the idea of an Inner Wolf (or in Lee's case, an Inner Pig) convincing. But there is another possible explanation, more clearly biological, of why the stories of our lives are so frequently opaque to us. This second explanation is that the rules for how we have relationships seem to be represented in our brains using implicit rather than explicit memory. Implicit, or procedural, memory is the type of memory with which we learn how to ride a bicycle or a new tennis serve. We use implicit memory when we learn a new skill, gain knowledge about how to do something specific, learn a procedure. As you will realize if you think about riding a bicycle or learning a new serve, acquiring the implicit memory of a procedure requires practice. But once we have learned the skill, it becomes virtually automatic, and we do not have to think through the steps involved. We "just do it." And as the old saying goes, once you know how to ride a bike, you never forget. Implicit memories often begin with explicit rules. You learn to shift bicycle gears by remembering which lever moves which set of gears and by concentrating on how fast you are pedaling. But by the time you hit the Tour de France, chances are you no longer think about it when you change gears.

In contrast to implicit memory, explicit memory is the type of memory with which we record specific events or facts—for example, a particular roller-coaster ride, or who is president at the moment. This type of memory often takes no more than one trial for learning to occur. So if I tell you that pigs have teeth, you are likely to know that they do the next time the subject comes up, which may not be for quite a while. Not many people learn to ride a bike flawlessly in one trial.

Although Freud emphasized the exploration of explicit

childhood memories during psychoanalysis, implicit learning probably is more important in forming and changing our representations of ourselves and others. In other words, learning how to have a relationship is more like learning to ride a bike than like memorizing all fifty state capitals. Although a patient near the end of treatment often looks back at our relationship and recalls moments that stood out—shared bits of humor, times when I did things he didn't think I would do, experiences of insight and mutual understanding when everything seemed to come together—I believe it is my being there day in and day out, and consistently trying my best to understand, that has really changed his mind. To quote Woody Allen, and in keeping with Stern's findings, 90 percent of life is showing up.

There is good evidence to suggest that the biology underpinning implicit memory is distinct from that underlying explicit memory. Implicit memory is encoded slowly and directly into the cerebral cortex itself through the incremental shifting of connections between neurons. In contrast, when we form an explicit memory for a specific event or fact, the event makes a big and immediate first impression in our hippocampus (a part of the brain concerned with specific memories), laying down a distinctive memory trace. This memory trace is gradually transferred to the cortex for long-term storage. The hippocampal portion of the brain is essential for explicit memory, the storing of new facts and life events, as was colorfully demonstrated by one well-known patient, HM.

HM's hippocampus was removed to treat his intractable seizure disorder, but this surgery produced a severe side effect: After the operation, HM could not store new experiences and facts. He would be told the names of his doctors over and over every day, yet he would never be able to remember them for more than a few minutes. Even with this severe impairment in his episodic memory, however, HM still had intact implicit memory. He learned mirror drawing, which involves learning to copy a figure by looking at a reflection of what you are drawing rather than looking at it directly. A seemingly useless skill (why couldn't HM's researchers have taught him to bowl instead, I wonder?), mirror drawing nevertheless takes practice to master, because it depends on being able to transpose the figure left to right and to use the mirror image as a guide. HM slowly became better at mirror copying with practice. In fact, he learned to mirror draw as well and as quickly as people without hippocampal damage. Of course, every day when his experimenters would ask him if he had ever seen the mirror-drawing task before, HM would say no.

The idea that we encode our rules about how to have a relationship slowly and directly into the cortex, using our implicit memory mechanisms, makes sense for a number of reasons. First, modern memory research suggests that children do not even have intact explicit memory until the third to fourth year of life, because the pathways involved in the hippocampus are not yet fully developed. This fits with my clinical observations about the memories of events that patients bring to psychotherapy; despite Freud's interest in early life, specific memories from the first three or four years are usually few and far between. Yet clearly things that matter happen in relationships in the first four years of life, so it seems likely that we learn how to approach relationships with other people through the daily practice we receive within our families.

A second line of data, from neural network research, suggests that self and other representations are implicit and change slowly over time in response to experience. In training a neural network, researchers have found it best to change the weights between neurodes very slowly. They shift a network a bit in the direction of a new experience rather than entirely remodeling it based on one new input. If a neural network were radically shifted by a single episode, the analogue of explicit memory, it would not be a true representation, because the single new experience would cancel out all prior patterns. Researchers have learned that networks are more stable and form better overall representations of experience when they shift very gradually in response to experience. Our representation of the Cheshire Cat arises from this slow shifting of neuronal connections where examples are averaged together over time.

If our model of how relationships work is stored primarily in implicit rather than explicit memory, it is stored as a process, a set of procedures. And if you think about other processes and procedures, you will quickly realize that we are not generally very good at making our knowledge of procedures explicit: we just know how to do them. In other words, our models for how to have relationships are opaque to us in the same way that our models of how to ride a bike are. It is difficult to be specific about what we understand about the nuances of riding a bike. If someone asks us how, we will probably have a hard time telling them how to do it beyond the basics. We have learned how to balance the bicycle around curves by practicing it. We cannot convey this information to someone else in words in a way that helps them master it without practice. Of course, some talented observers, such as coaches, are good at pointing out what is wrong with our forehand, rim shot, or field goal kick. They can tell us approximately what we are doing wrong and how to fix it. But fixing it still takes practice.

In this regard, psychotherapists are like coaches. Of course, part of what sports coaches do is watch films, enabling them and their players to see over and over what went wrong when they missed that field goal. This replaying of events over and over is similar to the repeated recognition of patterns typical of insight-oriented psychotherapy. But in sports, players generally are eager to know anything and everything that might improve their game. As we have seen from Shevrin and Bond's work on the unconscious, patients partly want to know their conflicts and partly want to hide them.

"I was on top of her," Lee says, as she starts to tell me about a recent sexual encounter with her girlfriend, two years after the dream of the BLT. "Suddenly I remembered that she has this fantasy about making love with a lion. So I leaned down and growled softly into her ear. I feel a bit silly telling you this. I mean it's stereotypical, lesbians and cats and all. But the truth is that I enjoyed becoming a lion for a moment. And I enjoyed the idea that I was spontaneously acting on her fantasy. And she liked it. So I guess it's not so silly after all."

With such shifts in Lee's feelings about her own desires, it is not surprising that she has been able to begin and maintain a mutually satisfying relationship with a woman. If there is one thing that Freud was right on the mark about, it was that psychoanalysis helps people to become more free and more fulfilled in work, love, and play. Lee's love life is clearly different, but so is her capacity for work and play. She has her house on North Carolina's Outer Banks, where she writes all summer and runs on the beach. She has a girlfriend with whom she has a meaningful and sexually gratifying relationship. She has greater access to feelings and fantasies that used to scare or distress her, and she can harness them in the service of her writing. And at some point late in her analysis, I begin to realize that her home at the beach is peopled not with friends, but with the characters of her new novel, as palpably real to her as my family, friends, and patients are to me.

Psychotherapy teaches us to understand and appreciate the story of our life that we have woven over time in images and symbols. Just as no snowflake has exactly the same shape as another, the story of our life is uniquely our own. Because there are certain experiences inherent in the human condition, there are common threads to the stories we tell, threads that bind us together in the tapestry of humanity. As a therapist I see these themes over and over in my daily work with patients: separating and merging, excluding and including, attaching and disconnecting, dominating and submitting, controlling and surrendering, possessing and coveting. There is a conflict built into each of these themes; separating makes you feel free and autonomous, but it can also make you feel all alone. Our various attempts to balance these dilemmas form the core of our most basic stories.

Whose Story Is It, Anyway?

Each of these themes can be played out with differing images and symbols. Like Stern's vitality affects, they are processes, ways of being—in this case, ways of being with others. Many core psychoanalytic myths can be revisited (and, I believe, freshened up) when seen from this perspective. For example, Freud's Oedipus complex is really a tale of possessing (of the mother by the father) and coveting (of the mother by the son, of what the father has). It is one version of a familiar plotline that arises from possession and envy. The covetous son tries to steal the mother, and his possessive father retaliates by stealing his most valued possession, his penis. Penis envy in women can be seen as the two-person version of this story, with the female coveting the penis and wanting to take it from the male. That Freud's central stories involved penises—which are, in fairness to the bearded forefather of psychoanalysis, a defining feature of the male-female dialectic—has hurt psychoanalysis as a field by making it reducible to phalluses, when possessing and coveting are probably more fundamental and powerful. These common human themes are played out by all of us in daily life with specific individual contents. The themes themselves form the equivalent of different film genres, which Roy Schafer has termed "master narratives." Carl Jung would call them Ur-stories, and Harry Stack Sullivan would suggest they arose from early interpersonal interactions.

As Lee and I begin to discuss ending treatment, she recounts that she read *The Prince of Tides* three times recently, almost compulsively. The story is set in coastal South Carolina, a landscape evocative of Lee's beloved Outer Banks. Tom, a coach and teacher in Charleston, has come to see his sister, a writer, in a New York hospital after a suicide attempt. He gradually helps her psychiatrist, Dr. Lowenstein—Barbra Streisand, in the movie—piece together the hidden childhood memory of rape and murder that is making his sister suicidally depressed. As they work together, the two affect each other's lives. Tom helps rescue Lowenstein's angry teenage son by being a kind father, teaching him things like how to play football. Dr. Lowenstein helps Tom to realize the value of his marriage and family and to recognize that home is the place where he belongs. The two have a love affair, which ends with a farewell night of dancing at the Rainbow Room.

Tom returns home a changed man, Lee recounts. She asks if I remember Tom's speech toward the end of the book, but I can't recall it. Lee rents the movie and watches it, pausing to write down the words she wants to bring to read to me in her session. She reports that Tom says:

> *In New York, I learned that I needed to love my mother and father in all their flawed, outrageous humanity. And in families there are no crimes beyond forgiveness. But it is the mystery of life that sustains me now. And I look to the North and I wish again that there were two lives apportioned to every man, and every woman. At the end of every day I drive through the city of Charleston, and as I cross the bridge that will take me home, I feel the words building inside me. I can't stop them or tell you why*

Whose Story Is It, Anyway?

I say them, but as I reach the top of the bridge, these words come to me in a whisper. I say them as prayer, as regret, as praise. I say, "Lowenstein, Lowenstein."

I hadn't been able to understand when I saw the movie why I liked it so much or cried so much at the end. Was it the swell of the violins? Was it Barbra? In fact, I felt a little disgusted with myself about liking the film because it was schmaltzy. It contained things like the boundary-bending affair between Lowenstein and Tom, something I always deplore in movies with psychiatrist characters, and the simplistic idea that the uncovering of old, forgotten memories is curative, which is a throwback to Freud's first (abreactive) model of the mind.

As Lee talks about the central secret—murder—which lay buried within the psyches of the two siblings, she compares it to her own powerful memory of the hog hanging from the tree, with its connections to her forbidden appetites and desires. At this point, something starts to stir within me, and I tune out for a moment, following my own string of associations. If Lee has incorporated a representation of me into her neural networks, one that will stay with her once we stop meeting, one that has truly changed her mind, it is also true that by this point I have a strong representation of her in my mind, brain, and heart as well. I think about the upcoming end of treatment, and it suddenly begins to dawn on me why I liked the movie. I remember the last scene, in which every day at sunset, as Tom journeys home, he invokes his powerful love for Lowenstein: "Her name springing to my lips, like poetry, like a prayer." She is clearly with him, though their relationship is over, and they each have had an impact on the other's lives in much the way that a successful psychotherapeutic relationship does. I realize I want Lee to think of me, feel connected to me, when this is all over. I feel attached to her as well. I think about the power, fun, and sometimes the scariness of being a therapist, about allowing another's mind to reverberate and ultimately take up permanent residence in mine. I wonder if my disgust at myself for liking the movie parallels Lee's disgust at herself about Helen and the dream of the BLT. I say to her, the session nearly at an end: "Perhaps the movie's ending, the way Lowenstein and Tom stay with each other once their relationship is over, has meaning as you and I talk about ending this treatment." Lee concurs, and we part ways for the day.

Only after this session ends do I muse about the fact that in *The Prince of Tides*, the psychiatrist is Jewish and the patient a WASP, a reversal of sorts of my relationship with Lee. And then I remember that Dr. Lowenstein's original patient, Savannah, Tom's sister, was writing a book with Holocaust themes using a Jewish pseudonym prior to her suicide attempt. At just the point where my curiosity is piqued, it occurs to me that Lee and I soon will be ending therapy, and that she will travel these side streets of her life narrative alone.

I recall my experiences at hang-gliding school in North Carolina, where I learned to launch myself off the sand dunes at Kill Devil Hills. I learned to fly in the shadow of Kitty Hawk, the town next door, Lee's stomping ground, the Outer

Banks. And I remember something an instructor told me that I found very hard to believe until I actually saw it with my own eyes. When the air currents come off the dunes just right, rising as the sand heats up, expert hang gliders can sometimes find an updraft that lifts them in an arching spiral up toward the clouds on a column of warm air. Leonardo da Vinci appreciated the power of flight, and so did the Wright brothers. All creative ventures, psychotherapy included, ultimately involve going with a process, letting it evolve. Learning to appreciate the processes by which our minds work enriches our inner lives and sends our spirits soaring. In my mind's eye I see Lee launch her Self on gossamer wings and soar off the dunes, out over the ocean.

8

An Analyst's Dream

I bought stock in Johnson & Johnson that appreciated dramatically over time. I was about to sell it to buy a red Saab Turbo convertible, when I woke up.

I have argued in this book that psychotherapy changes your brain. Dreams serve as a springboard, because of the unique way that they randomly express the most basic stories contained in our neural networks. These narratives are so consistent and repetitive in their core themes that they ultimately give structure to even the chaotic brain activity of dreaming sleep. Neural network models demonstrate that interlinking networks of neurons can indeed give rise to interconnected ideas. Changing the strength of the neural connection alters the way in which ideas are interconnected. Kandel's sea slugs showed that individual neural circuits can change in response to experience, a phenomenon that explains on a cellular level how the human brain learns in response to the experience of psychotherapy.

When many of these changes occur in particular neural circuits, parts of the brain responsible for particular representations can be permanently changed. Even adult brains are remarkably plastic, shifting dramatically in a manner consistent with how they are being used, suggesting that if we repeatedly attack ingrained and problematic representations of self and other, we can actually alter our relationship templates over time.

Stern's work suggests both that early perceptual experiences drive the formation of prototypes and that humans are prewired to form relationships with others. And the role that early relationships play in literally forging the brain circuits for affective self-regulation highlights how closely our views of self and other are linked to the emotional timbre of those relationships. This interplay of attachment and emotion in early life is important, gradually teaching us to tolerate intense feeling-states and to regulate them ourselves. It is often disturbances in our early life experiences that result in problems of self-esteem, attachment, and dysregulation of painful moods that bring most patients to intensive psychotherapy.

It fascinates me that neurobiologists and psychoanalysts have arrived at the same term—structural change—for describing what happens in psychotherapy. Of course, neurobiologists define structural change as shifting neuronal connections, while psychoanalysts refer to changing structures of the mind such as the ego. Still, the parallel word choice is interesting. I wish psychoanalysts would adopt a neurobiological term—exuberant growth (which refers in neural science to the rapid sprouting of new neural connections)—to describe what they are trying to promote in psychotherapy.

At first I am puzzled about my reasons for having stock in Johnson & Johnson. And I am certainly disappointed to see my red sports car fade away. But as I think about it, what stands out about the stock in my dream is that it is a blue-chip, growth-oriented choice, one whose dividends almost certainly will increase over time. It is a "buy and hold" kind of investment; owning this stock requires a measure of determination, the willpower to stick with it through the market's ups and downs. I recall reading recently that Johnson & Johnson has a DRIP, a direct reinvestment plan, which would allow me to purchase additional shares of the stock without a broker after my initial investment.

I begin to see that my dream is a metaphor for how I think about the process of psychotherapy. The purchase itself is like the investment in time, money, and energy that we make in psychotherapy. Indeed, the process of choosing a therapist involves literally choosing one's company for the journey ahead. Choosing a growth-oriented blue-chip stock, like choosing a good therapist, is important in assuring a dividend. But choosing good stock does not mean that the road will not get rocky; in all treatments, as with most long-term investments, it takes determination to stay the course when the going gets tough. Even when psychotherapy doesn't seem to be paying off, if you believe in your choice of investment you can ride out the ups and downs with the reasonable hope that ultimately you will achieve your goals. And if you give up on your therapy at the first signs of difficulty, you will probably be selling it—and yourself—short.

As I have tried to show, because changing your brain is a cell-by-cell process, psychotherapy really can substantially change your mind only over time. And while psychotherapy usually has its ups and downs, I believe you should experience fairly steady, readily apparent dividends along the way.

As things progress in therapy, there is indeed the psychotherapeutic equivalent of direct reinvestment of dividends: you begin to acquire additional insight and to make changes on your own, without your therapist. Successful psychotherapy fosters the capacity for self-analysis, a direct reinvestment that allows you to end psychotherapy yet continue to progress, to apply the self-understanding gained through working with your therapist to new life situations as they arise. Then you are able to afford your sports car and you are capable of enjoying it, too.

My model of mind and brain suggests several mechanisms through which psychotherapy leads to change. First, psychotherapy helps us to gain self-awareness about the story our cortical synthesizer contains. By observing the flow of our ideas, we begin to see the recurrent patterns and to recognize the signposts that suggest we are going down a particular well-worn path. This self-recognition, known as insight, often happens relatively early in treatment as we work with our therapists to characterize the recurrent themes of the stories of our lives. Insight often is initially frustrating, because once we see what we are doing, why can't we just cut it out? Our story synthesizer is so strongly ingrained in our cortex that it shapes the chaotic neural activity of REM sleep into dreams. Recognizing its main patterns is a necessary, but not sufficient, ingredient of change.

A second path to change in psychotherapy is the slow accretion of shifting connections between neurons as we find and challenge our usual operating modes in relationships. Our typical approaches to relationships come into focus as we examine how we relate to our therapists as our treatment unfolds. It is recognizable also in other important relationships in our lives, past and present. Examining what we do in different relationships over time helps to reshape our minds the way doing different arm exercises at the gym remakes our bodies. By repeating the same pattern over and over in our relationships, we theoretically build up huge biceps, for example, while our triceps and deltoids wither. Just as having well-developed triceps or deltoids gives us a wider range of potential uses for our arms, examining, restructuring, then applying the patterns our story synthesizers usually resort to make our relationships stronger and more flexible as well.

Intensive psychotherapy works also by allowing our encoded patterns to come to life in full force through the relationships with our therapists. This reawakening and re-experiencing of the core patterns gives us a chance to really work on our prototypes of self and other, questioning their hidden assumptions and presumptions about reality one by one, and in the process defanging them.

This laborious process of rewiring the brain's representations occurs alongside a third mechanism of change in psychotherapy: as we explore the ways in which we see our therapists through the lens of the past, we are also forming new relationships. Through the powerful corrective emotional experience of our relationships with our therapists, we remake our views of ourselves and others in relationships. Taking the therapist into the network of interlinking neurons that makes up your mind—comprises your story synthesizer—gives you a new and different relational other or character to play with, frequently a more reliable, more accepting one than you have experienced in daily life.

Our relationships with our therapists build and help us internalize new models of how relationships can work. Though the therapeutic relationship itself is not sufficient to change your mind, it is crucial that gaining insight and exploring the old patterns occur in the context of this new and different interaction with an important other.

A fourth mechanism of change in psychotherapy arises from the fact that our lives continue while we are in treatment, giving us a chance to practice what we are learning in psychotherapy over and over again in situations outside the psychotherapy session. Like a piano student who thinks about and works on a particular piece that he has played and will play again for his teacher, the person in psychotherapy needs to practice on a daily basis. Practice is essential because it magnifies the impact of each lesson and gives us a better chance of retaining and using the things we are learning.

Finally, psychotherapy works because it involves our experiencing of intense and often painful affects as they arise when we explore the past and the present, in the context of our prototypes of ourselves and others. Seeing that we do not die or disintegrate when we experience intense anger, anxiety, sadness, shame, or excitement gives us a growing capacity to experience emotions more fully while feeling more capable of modulating our own emotional reactions. We may have missed out on the amplification of elation we needed in the first year of life. If so, then therapy will help by making our capacity to experience joy and elation greater. We may have had caretakers whose approach to teaching us self-restraint left us ashamed and humiliated, lacking the ability to repair a relationship—and our own self-esteem—once it is ruptured. If so, then psychotherapy will help us to feel less ashamed and less inhibited. We will begin to experience relationships as less fragile. Overall, our capacity for an expanded range of affects and our growing ability to regulate them will help to make the tapestry of our lives richer, brighter, and more pleasurable.

You might be feeling a little skeptical of my interpretation of my own dream. After all, we've seen that dreams are over-determined, with multiple levels of meaning embedded in their imagery. Perhaps my Johnson & Johnson–stock dream is more than just a handy psychotherapy metaphor that presents itself at the moment when I need it. As I think further about Johnson & Johnson, I recall that my mother used to wash my hair with No More Tears baby shampoo, then brush and towel dry it, every Saturday, getting me ready for church on Sunday morning. I remember it frustrated her that I kept putting my head down, sticking my nose back into whatever book I was lost in at the moment. Reading while she dried my hair was my own form of protest; she was convinced that brushing and towel drying my hair made it more shiny than letting it dry naturally, but I would have been happier shining less and reading more. Looking back on it, I am touched at the energy she put into taking care of me, helping me look my best all those years. And while I may not have come away from church with the religious message as firmly etched into my brain as my mother might have hoped, it was there that I first heard and grew to love classical music. I liked the sanctuary in the summer, when Bible school and hymn sing-alongs took place. I think about how my mother would cry at "The Old Rugged Cross," her father's favorite hymn, which was played at his funeral shortly before I was born. It is a great regret of hers that he never got to see me. But this image of my mother's tears leads me back further still to my maternal grandmother and great-grandmother. In photographs, Grandmother Hill looks rather somber in her chair, with my sister and me perched tentatively at her side. She had a bad case of depression in a day when there was no effective treatment for it. In the end she took to bed, and she asked my mother to stay home with her for an extra year after high school. It is probably another of my mother's regrets that she said yes. Perhaps my grandmother was herself just repeating a familiar pattern, for she too had stayed behind with Great-Grandmother Taylor, who also was depressed. I think it was probably these intergenerational depressions and their effects on my family that led me toward a career in psychiatry in the first place. I realize with a start that "Saab" is a homonym for "sob."

As you've read the stories throughout this book, I hope you've formed a picture of how psychotherapy looks, sounds, and feels when all is going well. Furthermore, I hope that you will be able to make use of this picture, to apply it directly to your own experiences in psychotherapy.

First and foremost, do you trust your therapist enough to be willing to take him or her into the very fiber of your being? Into the neural networks that make up your mind? After all, you're going to allow the therapist to be carried around in your head for the rest of your life.

Many therapists would like to pretend that with proper technique, any therapist can work with any patient. This clearly is not true. I wouldn't randomly seat people next to each other at a dinner party, and I wouldn't indiscriminately introduce two friends just because they both are single. I'd want to have some gut-level feeling that they would hit it off. In fact, the gut-level feeling two people get when they really connect may even suggest they have complementary or at-tuned neural networks in the first place. Choosing a thera-pist is more important than a dinner party or a blind date for many reasons, not the least of which is that psychotherapy lasts much longer. And while it's true that you can't pick your parents, you can choose your own therapist. You'll want to pick who you snuggle up to carefully.

My model of psychotherapy also suggests that to really

change, you have to focus on recognizing the same patterns or themes in situation after situation. This means work. Pattern recognition is at the heart of psychotherapy; the active focusing and connecting of ideas and emotions that it requires is a necessary step that directly affects the structure of your brain. If I am afraid of dogs and really want to get over my fear, I cannot just wait to randomly encounter dogs and hope that this will change my mind. I have to systematically face dogs in increasingly nearer, more intense ways until I am no longer afraid. The same goes for relationships. Meandering in your networks may be valuable in uncovering the patterns that they contain, but it is not enough to really change your mind.

In informing you about the effects of psychotherapy on the brain, I have also attempted to show how some of Freud's most fundamental ideas—free association, dream interpretation, exploration of the patient-therapist relationship (the transference), emphasis on the importance of early life—make sense in terms of what we now know about the functioning of the brain. But even if free association and the exploration of the transference make sense in neural terms, they rarely seem natural to patients in psychodynamic psychotherapy.

Let's face it, it is bizarre to tell your most intimate secrets to a therapist about whom you know relatively little *factual* information. I stress factual because I do believe that you come to know a good deal about your therapist as a person with a distinct way of looking at the world, an individual cognitive and emotional style, a particular sense of humor. But therapy is very different from our usual social modes of functioning, and it is uncomfortable at first.

The relative anonymity of the therapist helps to facilitate the evolution of the transference. Because we often don't know exactly what our therapists really think, we can let the story lines implicitly contained in our neural networks become explicitly expressed in the relationships with our therapists. The popular, parodic version of this Freudian position of anonymity, which I call the therapist-as-Mount-Rushmore mode of psychotherapy, is one in which a patient continuously is met with silence on the part of the therapist. It's my feeling that relative anonymity which serves to foster the transference is one thing; stonefacing a patient is another.

In one study, therapists admitted that they themselves chose therapists who were active, not silent, during their own sessions. So don't feel bad if you want your therapist to talk more during your sessions; your therapist probably wants his therapist to talk more, too. And as a therapist, my goal is not to use the least possible number of words in any given session. Even if I decide not to answer a question a patient poses, I will often explain why I am not answering. I feel that the bond between patient and therapist is too important to let it be encroached upon by an overly silent analytic stance, which patients often perceive as withholding. After all, psychotherapy is about relationships, not power struggles and mind games.

I have tried also to highlight how psychodynamic therapy's emphasis on early life makes sense in terms of what

Freud called stereotype plates, which I have termed prototypes. It is these first interactions with others that serve as the
scaffolding on which later relationships are built. However,
this does not mean that psychotherapy is a fault-seeking mis-
sion in which the goal is to blame your parents for all your
problems—although this is how it often is perceived. My favorite example of this pitfall of psychodynamic treatment is
a *New Yorker* cartoon in which a cat is lying on an analytic
couch, saying, "I can still hear my mother's harsh voice:
'What, lost your mittens, you naughty kittens . . . then you
shall have no pie.' "

In one sense, the argument that I have proposed about how
psychotherapy changes your brain represents the pendulum's
ultimate swing toward biology, toward explaining in neural
terms what happens between two people in a psychotherapy
session. In another sense, my argument can be seen as the ultimate pro-psychological position as well, since psychotherapy may be the main, if not the only, way to affect the
representations of relationships that make up your mind.

If the early part of this Decade of the Brain was the Age
of Prozac, the latter part of the 1990s may consist of an over-
due correction in how we construct our selves. Our current
construction of the self, rooted in biology, gives rise to the
fatalistic idea that behavior such as violence is programmed
in our genes. Thus we can shrug off our shortcomings because our behavior operates beyond our control and so is not
our fault. Naturally, this perspective is accompanied by a
shift in our belief about which psychiatric treatments are

likely to work and why. Of course, not all aspects of the bio-
logicalization of the self are bad; the implications of moral
failure that used to accompany depression, and the patients'
beliefs that if they were determined enough they could pull
themselves out of these states, were harmful and incorrect.

Still, it is ironic that we believe we have little ability to
change ourselves psychologically in the era of the personal
trainer. I find that sometimes when I suggest that patients
come to treatment more often, even those who can afford it
balk. But remember, four 45-minute psychoanalysis sessions
amount to three hours a week—less than 3 percent of your
time devoted to changing your mind. Many people spend
more time than this at the gym acquiring washboard abs, and
think nothing of it.

There are philosophical implications of the model I have
proposed for how psychotherapy changes your brain as well.
My model calls into question some fundamental ideas about
human existence, such as the belief that we all are alone in
our own skins. Given the idea that one person can function
as a regulator of another's brain chemistry and structure, can
we really believe that we live and die so fundamentally separated from one another? With our new understanding of the
brain, the once clear-cut lines between inside and self versus
outside and other begin to blur.

Psychotherapy allows us to have an intense relationship
with another person, to construct a story about ourselves, to
change our minds and brains. Psychotherapy provides a route
through which one can achieve exuberant growth, structural
change. But the power of the therapeutic relationship to ef-

fect change has implications for other relationships as well. I have seen patients in psychotherapy who form relationships with significant others that seem to spur their growth in new directions, often because each person seems to bring to the relationship a willingness to talk and work through issues that are troubling them.

It suggests also that your mother was right when she was worried about you being "in with the wrong crowd," when she asked you to be careful who you "associate with." And perhaps we ought also to be more careful about who we work for and with; maybe that ranting and raving boss or backbiting co-worker is doing more to you than just raising your blood pressure. Not only do the personalities and approaches to relationships of others around us rub off on us; over time, they probably cause much deeper changes as well.

The view of relationships and psychotherapy I have proposed suggests also the crucial importance of treating children well, of doing our best to show them how to have mutually meaningful and respectful relationships with other people. As parents, we are the first to make up our children's minds about how relationships work, teaching them indirectly through how we act with them and others. If learning to have a relationship is a function of implicit memory, more like riding a bicycle than memorizing state capitals, there is all the more reason to suspect that children will do as we do, not as we say.

In this high-tech age, our appreciation for the importance of human relationships is perhaps at an all-time low. Even as "personal communication" devices abound, and we all run around with beepers and cellular phones attached to one ear, sending faxes and e-mails, we probably have less time and energy for human contact and intimacy than ever before. Though the Internet, the World Wide Web, and the global economy make the world a smaller place, they do not necessarily make us closer to one another. We talk to one another's answering machines and sometimes are disappointed when we reach a person directly. We are disgruntled to find we have to use a teller rather than a machine at the bank. As more people work from home, and as family ties dissolve, our sense of isolation and loss of community is likely to grow. Evidence for increasing rates of anxiety disorders and depression abounds, and researchers ask why. Is it not possible that the growing distance among people is itself responsible? Thinking back to the effects of separation on rats and the natural social structures of primates, might it not be that as evolving technology weakens our links to one another by limiting our needs for person-to-person, face-to-face contact, we have put ourselves at risk for anxiety and depression?

I may have lost my Saab when I woke up, but I still can daydream about it. I imagine myself at the wheel, about to embark on a journey through a beautiful landscape with a craggy coastline, a blue sky capped like a cappucino with fluffy white clouds. When I think about why I want a red car, I find myself musing about Ted and his red boat. Perhaps my wish for the red car is a sign of my desire to feel that I, like Ted, have arrived. By summertime, after thirty years of school beginning at age three, I'll be done following the road map that led me to what must be one of the world's best professions. As a psychiatrist and psychoanalyst, my daily work—the exploration of patients' minds—is challenging. There are enough overlapping patterns in how different people work to make it possible for me to improve as a therapist with experience and training. Yet psychiatry was fascinating to me the first day I began learning about it, and it has become only more so the better I have become at it. There are not many jobs that get more and more interesting the longer one does them. I think of Rob and his apprenticeship to the sorcerer, how his fears about the stern old man masked his discomfort with his own sexual feelings. Maybe thinking about my own shiny red car in terms of success at work distracts me from other possibilities as well. In my dream, the car is curvaceous and rather sexy, and I feel that way driving it, too.

And why a Saab? It isn't the most expensive car around, though it is a very nice one. It's hard to explain why it appeals to me. Perhaps it's that it's offbeat, a kind of anomaly, not German or Japanese or American, not a BMW or a Mercedes, not a Lexus or an Infinity, not a Cadillac or a Lincoln Continental. I can almost smell the leather of the interior, and I imagine strapping my bike in the summer and my skis in the winter to the back of my car and escaping the city, turbo engine roaring. Perhaps in being a bit offbeat and turbo-charged, the car mirrors something about me, my rather scattered interests and my energy and drive. Driving fast is my equivalent of Lee's running on the beach; less athletic, perhaps, but equally exhilarating.

An Analyst's Dream

I find myself thinking that when my own psychoanalysis ends, I will actually be able to afford a red Saab convertible. It is a prospect that I'm surprised to find myself entertaining. When I started analysis, it was hard to imagine that there would come a time when it would be all right with me for it to end. Like Chris, I too had some uncertainty about whether it was worth getting attached to my analyst only to have to endure the pain of giving him up someday. As Chris's treatment continued, he began to feel it was worth it to have Astro. Even though the dog would eventually die, Chris could imagine the pleasure of years of company outweighing his pain.

If I had the Saab, I'd love to be out driving it now, just as the first signs of spring are appearing, and the air, even in New York, has the delicate scent of fresh greenery. I think of taking Alice for a ride, hoping she'll have come to appreciate that life is short and must be drunk of deeply and passionately, that it can be fun as well as frightening to bungee-jump off her mountain and into the fray. And I think about Katie, too. Her treatment ended recently, and I'm wondering whether she still feels comfortably connected to me as she moves on, recognizing that neither of us has gotten hurt and that attachments are perhaps less fragile, less easily shattered than she thought.

As I put on my sunglasses and pull out onto the West Side Highway, Manhattan appears in my rearview mirror. I watch as the light makes the glass and chrome of the buildings sparkle. I reach down and turn on the radio, and Frank Sinatra croons "Fly me to the moon . . ." I remember Frances's annoyance at the idea that she'd "got me under her skin," her humorous image of me and Prozac fused together, both coursing through her veins.

By now the backseat of the car seems crowded with a mixture of mothers and grandmothers, patients and family, friends and colleagues cheered by the ride. I feel surrounded and embraced, stretching for a moment in the warmth of the new spring sun. Is that a baby seat I see in the back? Perhaps another meaning of my Johnson & Johnson dream. I find myself thinking of the closing scene in *Interview with the Vampire*, where Tom Cruise crosses over the George Washington Bridge—or was it the Golden Gate?—in a convertible. I guess it's a way of reminding myself that I have the Wolf Within onboard, too.

As I glance to my right at the passenger seat, I see the faint, shimmering outlines of a person. My analyst materializes, sitting beside me. He is smiling, apparently enjoying the ride. I chuckle to myself when I realize that the fact that I bought a car with a stick shift will not escape his attention. I recall that once, early in my analysis, I complained bitterly about the term "auto-castration" being bandied about freely in my psychoanalytic class. I groused that it had irritated me to see the rich clinical material we had been studying reduced to such a pat psychoanalytic phrase. The next day I locked my keys in my car and missed most of my analytic session. "Auto-castration?" my analyst asked when I arrived late, irritated with myself. "More like a failure of auto-nomy," I replied. We both had a good laugh.

It is quiet now except for the radio and the hum of the

Saab's turbo engine, but the silence between us is comfortable. So, I think, he's finally sitting beside me instead of in back of me. I feel closer to being his colleague, like I've begun to move on from my apprenticeship phase. I remember the thrill of learning to ride my first bike, my father running behind me, holding on until I got the hang of it and then letting go, sending me on my way when he saw I was ready. I can picture my mother watching me proudly from the porch and clapping, almost as if it were yesterday.

I am finally in the driver's seat as an analyst and as an autonomous person who can set my own course. It delights me to think that I can help my patients reach this point as well. As we pass a billboard I must have seen a hundred times before, I notice with a start that it's an ad for Saab. "Find your own road!" it exclaims in splashy red letters. No wonder I like the car, I think, surprised and happy to make this connection between my new Saab and my new autonomy.

I glance toward my analyst, eager to tell him, wondering if he's also noticed the billboard and made this connection himself, but he's no longer there.

And yet he is.

Further Reading

The following brief list of books pertaining to the topics I have presented is intended as a guide for exploring areas of interest, not an exhaustive list of references.

CHAPTER 1: PUTTING THE NEURON BACK IN NEUROSIS

Hobson, J. Allan. *The Dreaming Brain*. New York: Basic Books, 1988.
Luborsky, Lester, and Paul Crits-Christoph. *Understanding Transference: The CCRT Method*. New York: Basic Books, 1990.
Miller, Laurence. *Freud's Brain: Neuropsychodynamic Foundations of Psychoanalysis*. New York: Guilford Press, 1991.

CHAPTER 2: IN SEARCH OF THE CHESHIRE CAT

Caudill, Maureen, and Charles Butler. *Naturally Intelligent Systems*. Cambridge, MA: MIT Press/Bradford, 1990.

Further Reading

McClelland James L., David E. Rumelhard, and the PDP Research Group. *Parallel Distributed Processing.* 2 vols. Cambridge, MA: MIT Press/Bradford, 1986.

Fuster, Joaquin M. *Memory in the Cerebral Cortex: An Empirical Approach to Neural Networks in the Human and Nonhuman Primate.* Cambridge, MA: MIT Press/Bradford, 1995.

Reiser, Morton F. *Memory in Mind and Brain.* New York: Basic Books, 1990.

CHAPTER 3: THE SEA SLUG ON THE COUCH

Kandel, Eric R., James H. Schwartz, and Thomas M. Jessell. *Essentials of Neural Science and Behavior.* Norwalk, CT: Appleton & Lange, 1995.

Schachter, Daniel L. *Searching for Memory.* New York: Basic Books, 1996.

Squire, Larry R., and Nelson Butters. *Neuropsychology of Memory,* 2d ed. New York: Guilford Press, 1992.

CHAPTER 4: TEACHING AN OLD DOG NEW TRICKS

Fuster, Joaquin M. *Memory in the Cerebral Cortex: An Empirical Approach to Neural Networks in the Human and Nonhuman Primate.* Cambridge, MA: MIT Press/Bradford, 1995.

Kosslyn, Stephen M., and Oliver Koenig. *Wet Mind: The New Cognitive Neuroscience.* New York: Free Press, 1995.

Stern, Daniel N. *The Interpersonal World of the Infant: A View from Psychoanalysis and Developmental Psychology.* New York: Basic Books, 1985.

CHAPTER 5: AN AFFECTIVE APPRENTICESHIP

Gazzaniga, Michael S. *The Cognitive Neurosciences.* Cambridge, MA: MIT Press/Bradford, 1995.

Further Reading

CHAPTER 6: THE MADONNA OF THE PROZAC CAPSULE

Kagan, Jerome. *Galen's Prophecy: Temperament in Human Nature.* New York: Basic Books, 1994.

Roose, Steven P., and Robert A. Glick. *Anxiety as Symptom and Signal.* Hillsdale, NJ: Analytic Press, 1995.

Schafer, Roy. *Retelling a Life: Narration and Dialogue in Psychoanalysis.* New York: Basic Books, 1992.

CHAPTER 7: WHOSE STORY IS IT, ANYWAY?

Miller, Nancy E., Lester Luborsky, Jacques P. Barber, and John P. Docherty, eds. *Psychodynamic Treatment Research: A Handbook for Clinical Practice.* New York: Basic Books, 1993.

Person, Ethel S. *By Force of Fantasy: How We Make Our Lives.* New York: Basic Books, 1995.

Index

Index

Index

Index

Index

patient's wishes and, 15
as pattern recognition, 38, 188
repetition in, 97, 98–99
silent analytic stance in, 189
story patterns in, 15–16, 159–63,
  172–73, 182–83, 189
therapist-patient relationship in, 4,
  183–84, 188–89, 191–92
therapist's relative anonymity in,
  188–89
therapist's representation formed in,
  123, 147–52, 175–76
time spent in, 98–99, 191
transference in, 14, 188, 189
vitality affects in, 93–94
working through in, 46–47

Rats, separation anxiety in, 133,
  136–37, 139, 193
Reflexes, 58
Relationships, 25, 56, 71, 77–101, 188,
  190, 191–93. *See also* Caretaker-
  infant relationship; infant
  development
  prototypes of. *See* Prototypes
  as story patterns, 15, 17
  therapist-patient, 4, 183–84, 188–89,
  191–92
REM (rapid eye movement) sleep,
  8–13, 17–18, 28, 33, 183
  intrusion of external information on,
  9–10
  neurobiology of, 8–11, 17–18
Reticular formation neurons, 9–13
  functions of, 9–11
  PGO waves generated by, 10–13,
  17
Retina, 31, 32
Rob (case history), 103–5, 109–14,
  118–21, 123–27, 194
Roose, Steven, 138
Rosenblum, Leonard A., 134
Rummelhart, David, 41
"Rush," 91

Schafer, Roy, 159, 173
Schore, Allan, 105, 106, 108, 115, 116,
  117–18, 122, 131, 132, 133
Sea slugs (*Aplysia californica*), learning
  by, 22, 57–62, 63, 66–68, 123,
  179–80
Self, 107, 122, 190–91
Self and other representations, 4, 18,
  79–80, 170, 180, 183–84, 191

complementary nature of, 111–12
detection of invariance in, 84
linked to positive emotions, 114
in Siamese twins, 83–84
Self-esteem, 122, 131, 132, 138, 139,
  180, 185
Self-image, 122, 133
Self-representations, 63–66, 68,
  72–75
Sensitization, 59, 61, 66, 67–68
Separation anxiety, 118, 131–38
  deprivation vs., 137–38
  in monkeys, 134–35, 137, 193
  in rats, 133, 136–37, 139, 193
  unpredictability in, 135
Serial computers, 37–38
Serotonin, 143–44
Shame, 115–16, 118, 122, 185
Shevrin, Howard, 162, 171
Siamese twins, 83–84
Singer, Jerome L., 150
Sleep. *See* REM sleep
Sleep paralysis, 10
"Space Oddity" (Bowie), 85
Space program, 84–86
Spinal cord, 10, 58
Spitz, René, 88
Stereotyping, 43
Stern, Daniel, 81, 82–84, 91–92, 93, 94,
  98, 115, 135–36, 168, 173, 180
Story patterns, 12–22, 25–51, 153–77,
  179. *See also* Dreams
  "Alice in Neverland," 26–28, 35–37,
  45–51
  conflict in, 161–63, 172–73
  defense mechanisms and, 55,
  160–64
  dogs in, 77–80, 84–86, 88–91, 94–97,
  99–101
  explicit vs. implict memories and,
  167–71
  in Freud's work, 173
  opaqueness of, 159–64, 166–71
  in psychotherapy, 15–16, 159–63,
  172–73, 182–83, 189
  Sorcerer's Apprentice theme in,
  104–5, 119–21, 123–26, 194
  therapeutic outcomes and, 15–16,
  19–22
  water in, 26, 27–28, 35, 45
Story synthesizer, 17–22, 25, 28–35, 56,
  57, 79, 80–81, 142, 159, 182–83
Strauss, Mark S., 82
Sufi story, 26, 27–28, 35, 45

Index

About the Author

*"A psychiatrist is a person who goes to the Folies
Bergère and looks at the audience."*
—BISHOP MERVYN STOCKWOOD

Susan C. Vaughan, M.D., is an NIMH research fellow studying
long-term psychotherapy and psychoanalysis at the New York State
Psychiatric Institute, and a senior candidate in psychoanalysis at the
Columbia Center for Psychoanalytic Training and Research in New
York City. She received her B.A. magna cum laude in psychology and
social relations from Harvard College in 1985, and her M.D. from
the Columbia College of Physicians and Surgeons in 1989. She did
her psychiatric residency training in the department of psychiatry at
Columbia, where she served as chief resident in 1993. Vaughan also
has a private psychiatric practice in New York City.